EPHESIANS

UNLOCKING PAUL'S MESSAGE: OUR DIVINE IDENTITY

DON KEATHLEY

TWS | THE WRITER'S SOCIETY PUBLISHING

Paperback: ISBN 978-1-961180-45-1

TWS Publishing
Lodi, CA
www.thewriterssociety.online

CONTENTS

INTRODUCTION

Let's take a journey through the Book of Ephesians — a letter that, despite its brevity, holds deep treasures waiting to be unearthed by hearts willing to dig deep, hearts desiring to understand the richness of God's word in a way that transforms how we live, love, and interact with the world around us.

As we open to the first page of this letter, penned by Paul but inspired by the Holy Spirit, it's as though we're stepping into a well-lit room where every corner whispers divine mysteries and truths. Ephesians is a book of two halves, yet one heart. In its initial chapters, Paul lays down a breathtaking foundation of our identity in Christ — reminding us of the spiritual blessings we've been given, the grace we stand in, and who we are in Christ from before the foundation of the world.

It's easy to jump ahead, eager for practical advice and directives on how to live out who we are. Yet, Paul starts with revelation before moving to instruction, a reminder that our doing flows out of our being.

The first half of this book isn't just a preamble; it's the essence of what follows. Without a deep, internalized understanding of our identity and position in Christ, our efforts to live out Chapters 4, 5, and 6 risk becoming just that — efforts. A life of *doing* rather than expressions of a heart transformed by grace. But, oh, the transformation that awaits us when we truly grasp the depth of our identity in Christ!

This journey through Ephesians invites you into a living conversation with Paul, God, and yourself. It's a call to examine not just the words on the page but the heart behind them. As we dive into teachings on unity, love, and the whole armor of God let's carry the revelations of Chapters 1, 2, and 3 with us, allowing them to illuminate our path and guide our steps.

So, as you turn these pages, I encourage you to do so with an open heart and a spirit ready to be stirred. Let's not just seek knowledge but transformation. Whether you find yourself in a season of questioning, growth, or perhaps even challenge, may the truths within this book be a beacon, reminding you of God's unconditional love, the strength of His grace, and the call to live as your authentic self.

Together, let's explore the fullness of what it means to be in Christ — a journey not just of understanding but of manifesting His life in the world.

Welcome to the Book of Ephesians!

1

AWAKENING TO OUR INHERENT SONSHIP

A s we explore the book of Ephesians, you will recognize its significant relevance to the modern Western Church. In this chapter, we will examine verses 3 to 10 of Ephesians Chapter 1, which might challenge some long-held beliefs or introduce new perspectives you haven't considered before.

UNVEILING EVERY SPIRITUAL BLESSING WITHIN

Verse 3: "Blessed be the God and Father of our Lord Jesus Christ, who has already blessed us with every spiritual blessing in the heavenly places in Christ."

Recognizing that this blessing is expressed in the past tense is crucial. God has already abundantly poured out *every* spiritual blessing upon us. These heavenly realms are not distant; they reside within you, within the inner garden or kingdom of your being.

Paul doesn't stop there. He goes even deeper in verse 4, emphasizing that God chose us in Christ even before the world's foundation.

Verse 4: "Just as He chose us in Him before the foundation of the world, that we should be holy and without blame before Him in love."

This divine choice is not contingent on our actions but is rooted in love. Moving forward to verse 5, we see that we were predestined to be adopted as God's sons through Jesus Christ.

Verse 5: "Having predestinated us to adoption as sons by Jesus Christ to Himself, according to the good pleasure of His will."

It's important to note that this predestination isn't about our merits but is purely a result of His will. Continuing the thought, verse 6 beautifully tells us: "To the praise of the glory of His grace, by which He made us accepted in the Beloved." Our acceptance isn't earned through our efforts; it's a direct outcome of His limitless grace. In Christ, we are lovingly embraced and warmly welcomed into the Beloved.

Verses 7-9: "In Him we have redemption through His blood, the forgiveness of sins, according to the riches of His grace. Which He made to abound toward us in all wisdom and prudence. Having made known to us the mystery of His will, according to His good pleasure which He purposed in Himself."

Notice that it was a purposeful and deliberate act on God's part. It's not dependent on our efforts or comprehension.

Lastly, verse 10 unveils God's grand design.

Verse 10: "That in the dispensation of the fullness of the times –He might gather together in one all things in Christ, both which are in heaven and which are on earth—in Him."

What a glorious revelation! These verses collectively emphasize that everything Paul discusses is a testament to what God has accomplished rather than what we have achieved. It's a remarkable demonstration of God's grace and love, inviting us to wholeheartedly embrace and live within this reality.

In verses 3-10, Paul skillfully unveils the deep truths of our identity in Christ. His resounding message is crystal clear: We already possess every spiritual blessing generously bestowed upon us by God's good pleasure, by His divine purpose. There is nothing we lack.

Paul assures us that we already possess every spiritual blessing within us. There's no need to look externally or wait for the future; these blessings are already embedded in our inner being, ready to be realized. This perspective challenges long-held beliefs and upends traditional thinking. It moves us beyond the usual requests of asking for more or the habitual 'please give me' prayers we often rely on. Instead, it invites us to recognize and embrace the abundance within us, knowing that we lack nothing.

Peter said it a bit more strongly in 2 Peter 1:2. He stated, "Grace and peace be multiplied to you in the knowledge of God and of Jesus our Lord, as His divine power has given to us all things that pertain to life and godliness, through the knowledge of Him who called us by glory and virtue, by which have been given to us exceedingly great and precious promises, that through these you may be partakers of the divine nature, having escaped the corruption that is in the world through lust."

These spiritual blessings aren't just intangible concepts like joy or peace; they encompass all we need for life and godliness. Peter's expansion of the term aligns perfectly with Paul's Ephesian teachings. Together, they emphasize a life not of spiritual poverty but of abundance. If your prayers are dominated by a sense of lack, constantly begging God for what you think you're missing, it's time to shift that mindset.

UNLOCKING THE POWER OF IMAGINATION: ENGAGING WITH DIVINE CREATIVITY

Can you imagine that everything you need is already within your grasp? Your imagination is a powerful tool that bridges the gap between the spiritual and physical realms. When guided by the Holy Spirit, your imagination can see the things you already possess, whether they are necessities for life or elements of spiritual growth.

Paul spoke of every spiritual blessing, assuring us that we lack nothing. Take a moment to meditate and envision any need you currently face as already fulfilled. See yourself not only desiring but fully possessing what you seek. Imprint this mental image firmly in your imagination, and then cling to it steadfastly, regardless of any challenges that may arise. Even in the face of adversity, maintain a strong belief in its manifestation.

For example, if you're dreaming of starting a business, envision it vividly in your imagination. Picture yourself running it with success. Visualize every detail — the shop you'll work in, the office you'll occupy, the environment around you. Create as complete a picture as you can in your conscious mind. This process feeds your subconscious, which doesn't act independently but follows the conscious mind's lead. What you implant in your conscious mind seeps into your subconscious, and it's this content you'll begin to materialize in your life as long as you maintain a steady focus.

The hurdle many of us stumble upon is our tendency to lose sight of our dreams when faced with obstacles or unfavorable circumstances. It's easy to abandon our visions prematurely, feeling disheartened and defeated and wrongly concluding that our prayers have gone unanswered.

> But here's the truth: you have already been given everything necessary for life *and* godliness.

It's time to tap into that inner resource, draw from your subconscious, spirit, heavenly realm, kingdom, garden — or whatever you prefer to call it. The terminology isn't as important as seeing tangible results and witnessing the manifestation of your visions.

It's a process involving envisioning, speaking, and taking action. First, form the mental image within your consciousness, allowing your subconscious to absorb it. Next, affirm it with spoken words and follow through with concrete actions. All this is done in partnership with the Holy Spirit and your spirit — it's a Spirit-to-spirit partnership.

CHOSEN BEFORE THE WORLD BEGAN

Paul wastes no time dispelling any uncertainties about God's grace and favor. He begins by addressing the Ephesian Christians, who were not fully living up to their potential, with a powerful reminder: 'You have been blessed with absolutely everything by the Father.' Remember, he's teaching them who they are in Christ — this is something we need to drink of deeply.. In verse 4, he says, "Just as He chose us in Him before the foundation of the world, that we should be holy and without blame before Him in love." Paul's message is one of reassurance and security.

> He's telling them, *and by extension us* that our place has been firmly established. We were chosen, destined for this position, long before the world was formed. There should be no room for doubt about who we are in Christ.

Paul's message in Ephesians presents a unique perspective transcending theological debates like Calvinism and Arminianism. These later frameworks offer differing views on divine election and human free will. Calvinism suggests a predetermined selection, while Arminianism emphasizes individual choice in accepting Jesus. Calvinism is about the luck of the draw, and Arminianism is our personal choice in choosing Jesus.

Paul didn't shape the gospel to fit popular man-made theologies like Calvinism or Arminianism because he knew nothing of them. He wasn't concerned with Universalism either. All he knew and preached was the unadulterated truth of the gospel, the good news.

In the fourth verse, Paul unveils a foundational truth to the Ephesians *and us:* God chose us in Christ before the very foundations of the world were laid. This perspective shapes how we understand God seeing us. Our genuine identity is found in Christ, with whom we were co-crucified and co-resurrected.

Paul also beautifully articulates this concept in Colossians 3:1, where he advises, "If you were raised with Christ, seek those things which are above, where Christ is, sitting at the right hand of God. Set your mind on things above." By 'things above,' Paul isn't referring to distant or unreachable places or eternal destinations. He's urging us to focus our minds on matters of high spiritual significance, particularly on love, which he regards as the highest vibration in the universe.

In verse 3 of Colossians 3, Paul drives the point home: "For you died, and your life is hidden with Christ in God." The message is unmistakable: our thoughts should consistently dwell on 'throne-room realities,' concentrating on our unwavering position in Christ. When we firmly grasp this truth, we realize that nothing Adam did could alter God's sovereign plan. None of mankind's actions could ever dislodge us from our divinely appointed place. This understanding is paramount. It's not merely about redemption from past mistakes; it's about recognizing that our true position and genuine identity have always been secured in Christ, impervious to sin or any earthly transgressions.

Paul's imparting deep truths to the Ephesian Christians were not fully embracing their identity in Christ. Even after 2,000 years, we are still grasping the same truth: we are blessed with every blessing, chosen in Christ before the foundation of the world. For many of us, this revelation is entirely new because we haven't been taught to fully embrace who we are in Christ.

The focus in Western Christianity has been on accepting Jesus and once we do that *then* we are sons of God. To believe that we are accepted only after accepting Him contradicts what Paul wrote. It's a denial of the gospel, a position contrary to Christ. It's an antichrist stance. I know that might sound strong, but it's a reality — and it's time to challenge the status quo and kick over some sacred cows.

> " Understanding this is vital: Our acceptance by God isn't contingent on accepting Christ; God established His acceptance of us from the beginning.

This perspective may be challenging, but it's crucial for truly understanding the gospel.

PREDESTINED FOR SONSHIP

In verses 5 and 6, Paul further cements our *eternal* position in Christ.

Verses 5-6: "... having predestined us to adoption as sons by Jesus Christ to Himself, according to the good pleasure of His will, to the praise of the glory of His grace, by which He made us accepted in the Beloved."

Not only were we blessed with every spiritual blessing and chosen in Christ before the foundation, but Paul also declares that we were predestined for sonship. We were pre-wired as sons. And it was all God's doing — He didn't ask for our permission or decision. He did it according to the pleasure of His good will.

This revelation carries with it an overwhelming sense of security. Paul is unveiling the magnificence of our place within God's master plan. There are only two choices before us: to live in the provision given to us or to live by our own wits.

The message of Ephesians beckons us into a richer, more secure way of life. Calling us to recognize our predestined identity as beloved sons of God. However, many of us are still like the Ephesian Christians, relying solely on our abilities and not taking advantage of this deposit that was placed into our lives. We haven't grasped the concept of this inside-out living.

LIVING FROM THE INSIDE OUT

Much like the Ephesian Christians, many of us continue to navigate, life leaning heavily on our own understanding and efforts, largely overlooking the wellspring of spiritual resources within us. We haven't understood what it means to live from the inside out. Instead, we often operate from an external perspective, reacting to the ebb and flow of circumstances as they emerge, making choices grounded in immediate practicality rather than the deeper wisdom that lies within.

We were created to live, led by the indwelling Spirit. This Spirit-to-spirit connection or partnership should be the compass directing our external experiences. True spiritual living is about our inner reality shaping our outer experiences. When you live by your soul, you live by your emotions and rely on your willpower. All that stems from fear and insecurity comes from external sources. That's not the life we're meant to live. We're designed to live a life fueled by love, which originates from within.

Our purpose is to live a life filled with love that comes from deep within us. Love should serve as the wellspring from which our thoughts, actions, and responses naturally flow. When we choose to live in this manner, we are living more in sync with our intended design.

This way of life isn't reacting to the pressures exerted by external forces like fear and insecurity. Instead, it's empowered by an internal, enduring force — love. It represents a transformation from reacting to circumstances to proactively shaping them, from being influenced by the external world to governing from a place of inner strength and boundless love.

As we cultivate joy and nurture all the fruits of the Spirit within ourselves, we're developing this life of sonship, a life of ruling and reigning in grace. This requires a shift in focus from external to internal development. It took me years to fully understand and prioritize this inward-focused way of life, which revolves around cultivating these spiritual qualities. I encourage you to practice listening to that inner voice, to trust and rest in what your spirit is communicating.

Let's wholeheartedly embrace and practice this life of divine favor. As the saying goes, 'practice makes perfect.' So, don't be disheartened if you ever find yourself straying off course. God is always there, ready to gently guide you back. In my own journey, I haven't always been flawless in heeding His inner voice. There have been moments of missteps, but each time I faltered, I discovered that the Holy Spirit has consistently guided me back on track.

The Son and every subsequent son are called to live according to the Father's inner guidance — an inner knowing. Romans 8:14: "For as many as are led by the Spirit of God, these are sons of God." The operative word in this verse is 'led.' This isn't about being forcibly driven but being gently *led* by the Spirit. This distinction is elaborated upon in Romans 8:15, which states, "For you did not receive the spirit of bondage again to fear, but you received the Spirit of adoption by whom we cry out, 'Abba Father.'"

According to Paul's terminology, a son (or *huios* in Greek, signifying a mature son) of God is someone who is led by the Spirit, not driven by compulsion from the flesh and soul. Transitioning from fear to love is crucial.

Verse 16 of Romans 8 continues to shed light on this concept: "The Spirit Himself bears witness with our spirit that we are children of God." This verse highlights a partnership, a harmonious collaboration between the Holy Spirit and our spirit. For most of our lives, we've been accustomed to being guided by our minds, relying on our reasoning and emotions. However, as we mature into *huios*, becoming mature sons of God, we are transitioning to live from a deeper place within ourselves — where our spirit communes with the Holy Spirit.

EMPOWERED BY LOVE: SPIRIT LED LIVING

If you make a mistake, think of the Holy Spirit like a GPS in your car. Just like a GPS recalculates when you miss a turn, the Holy Spirit guides you even when you go off track. He's always there to help you get to your destination.

> Know this: You can never make a mistake that the Holy Spirit cannot correct!

I've spent countless hours praying and asking God to bless my path. Then, I found Proverbs 16:9, which says, "A man's heart plans his way, but the Lord directs his steps." This verse made me realize that, in the end, God guides me to where I need to be. I can get there by the hard route or the easy route. Following the Spirit makes the journey smoother.

Don't let the fear of making mistakes stop you from embracing a life led by the Spirit. This journey involves learning, growing, and receiving gentle guidance when necessary. It's about letting go of control and trusting the Holy Spirit, who is always within you. Paul is reassuring these Ephesians, and I'm reassuring you that there's nothing to fear in trusting the Holy Spirit to guide you. There is no fear in love.

John said it like this: "And we have known and believed the love that God has for us. God is love, and he who abides in love abides in God, and God in him." Then, in verse 17, it continues, "Love has been perfected among us in this: that we may have boldness in the day of judgment; because as He is, so are we in this world." To walk as Jesus did in this world, we must heed the guidance of the Spirit, just as the Spirit led Jesus.

After emerging from the waters of the Jordan following His baptism, Jesus transitioned from being a *teknon*, a child still growing in wisdom, stature, and favor with God and man, into a *huios*, a mature Son. Mature sons are led by the Spirit of God.

When faced with challenges or difficulties, we are reminded in this passage that there is no room for fear when love is present. Verse 17 emphasizes that love has reached its perfection among us, making us bold in the day of judgment. It's crucial to understand that this 'day of judgment' is not a future event where we stand before God as if watching a replay of our lives on a big screen. Instead, it could encompass our everyday moments when we must discern the right choices, making us bold because love inspires us. Let love guide you in those moments of judgment, empowering you to make resolute decisions with unwavering courage.

UNVEILING THE MYSTERIES OF REDEMPTION AND DIVINE PURPOSE

As we wrap up our look at Ephesians Chapter 1, let's dive into verses 7 through 10. These verses are important for understanding Ephesians 1:3-10, especially if you lead a Bible study or are helping others discover who they are in Christ. Ephesians is a valuable resource, particularly for those who may not fully grasp their spiritual inheritance in Christ.

Let's focus on verse 7, where Paul explores another remarkable aspect of what the Father has achieved for us, entirely independent of our efforts.

Verse 7: "In Him we have redemption through His blood, the forgiveness of sins, according to the riches of His grace."

The redemption and forgiveness of our sins are gifts from God, lavishly provided through His abundant grace — all His work, not ours.

Let's look at verses 8 to 10 for deeper insight:

Verse 8-9: "Which He made to abound toward us in all wisdom and prudence. Having made known to us the mystery of His will."

Paul's inviting the Ephesians, *and us,* to come up higher in our understanding. God is about to unveil a mystery to you, one that challenges some of your religious beliefs. He has revealed the mystery of His will according to His pleasure and purpose. This demonstrates God's deep love for us and His desire to walk closely with us as Father and son, guiding us into a deeper understanding of who we are in Christ.

So, in verse seven, he tells us that we've been redeemed, meaning we were fully represented in Christ. Since we're now free of all sins, we're absolved by the wealth of His grace. If your understanding of grace is not growing, you might still be wrestling with a lingering sense of sin consciousness.

I don't concern myself with other people's sins. I understand that sin carries consequences that aren't from God. However, God has taken care of the sin issue for us. We don't need to worry about it because of the abundance of His grace. Allowing grace to grow and expand eventually overwhelms any sense of sin consciousness.

Paul is emphasizing to the Ephesian Christians the value God places on them. Even more important is the value they should place on themselves, reflecting the work God has entrusted to them.

Part of learning to manifest as a son is being like Jesus. Just as Jesus saw Himself through the eyes of the Father, we, too, should see ourselves from His perspective. In Chapter 1, Paul outlines how God views us and how the Father has designed us to appear before Him: blameless, holy, and in love. He is saying that we should walk before Him or live a life free of guilt or condemnation. So, if that's how He sees us, we must see ourselves in the same way.

Verse 10: "That in the dispensation of the fullness of the times He might gather together in one all things in Christ, both which are in heaven and which are on earth — in Him."

As Paul concludes these ten verses, he unveils a profound mystery, a grand revelation: that at the end, when it's all said and done, God will gather everything together as one in Christ. This concept echoes Ephesians 2, where Paul tells us that we are God's masterpiece, crafted in Christ Jesus for good works that He has preordained. Every good work is already set in motion, part of His divine plan.

You might sometimes feel that your life hasn't amounted to much or accomplished significant things. However, I want to assure you that you are playing precisely the role you were meant to play. Your contribution is like a piece of a grand puzzle, and it matters. Your job, no matter how seemingly small, has its place. Each of us is a unique piece, and while some may be more visible or vocal, yours is just as crucial.

In fact, Philippians 2:9-11 beautifully reveals how it will all turn out. Every knee will willingly bow, and every tongue will joyfully confess that Jesus Christ is Lord, all to the glory of God. This confession isn't forced; it's a testament to the victory of love. Love triumphs in the end; it never fails.

The manifestation of the sons plays a pivotal role in bringing all of this to fruition. In verses 9 and 10, Paul is helping the Ephesian Christians to understand that they, too, have a significant part to play in this divine plan. The cloud of witnesses who have gone before us have also played their part. It all converges into this profound mystery so that, as Hebrews Chapter 10, verses 11- 14 tell us, Jesus offered His singular sacrifice for sins and then took His seat, patiently waiting until every enemy was placed under His feet.

MANIFESTING SONSHIP

Here's the incredible part: those feet are in the body of Christ, which includes you and me — the sons. We are the ones who will actively engage in placing every enemy under the authority of Christ.

> What's occurring today is significant: God is gradually withdrawing His hand from what He has designed for us to do. As He does so, He empowers His sons with full authority to step into action on Earth.

When we look around, especially at the challenges like Covid. It feels disheartening because we know it shouldn't be this way. Some might label it as God's judgment or the result of sin, but that's not the case. As manifested sons of God, the Father is revealing a unique opportunity to stand up and manifest His presence.

In times of distress, we, as sons, must embody peace, confidence, and hope. We stand against fear, guided by joy and peace. The turmoil in the world right now has many driven by fear, including some in the Christian and grace community. It's time for us to manifest our true identity as mature sons and counteract panic and fear with peace, joy, and love.

We are living out a different kingdom, one where we have unwavering confidence that our God meets every need. As we learn to rest in His presence and spend time in communion with Him, we become adept at being led by His guidance. He will assist us, revealing which river to cast our hook into to find the gold coin in the fish's mouth. This way of living is becoming our new norm.

This might sound bold to some, but let me share what I believe to be the absolute truth. God has already done everything He's going to do. He has provided us with everything He can provide. God is in a state of rest, waiting for His sons to manifest. He is awakening us to our true identity and all that we possess. We should no longer ask for what we already have, nor should we pray to become someone we already are. He is awakening us to our reality.

As God awakens us, He's gradually taking His hands off and entrusting us with His authority. Just as Jesus declared before His departure in Matthew 28:18, "All authority has been given to me in heaven and on earth." When He says **ALL,** He means **ALL** — His authority is the sole authority.

Then He commissions us, saying, 'I want you to go therefore.' He transfers His authority to us; it becomes our authority. In essence, our authority is His authority. He held nothing back from you. It's one unified authority under which we operate. Can you grasp the magnitude of this concept? It may stretch your imagination, but I encourage you to let it resonate in your mind. Fix that truth in your thoughts.

Moreover, in Hebrews 11:14, He has sanctified those being perfected. Objectively, we are already perfected, as we've learned from Ephesians. Subjectively, He is awakening, teaching, guiding, and leading us, and we are beginning to comprehend this objective reality.

What we should take away from these first 10 verses in Ephesians Chapter 1 is the full understanding that we are blessed with every spiritual blessing. This means we already possess everything we'll ever need. It's time to embrace our secure position, not just being placed in Christ but recognizing that we are inherently wired to be manifested sons.

The depth and degree of walking in sonship is entirely up to you. You can choose to walk in it as deeply as you desire. And as you venture deeper, God will continue to reveal more to you.

2

EMBRACING OUR DIVINE INHERITANCE

A couple of years ago, I did a series called "Embracing Your Divinity" that explored our authentic identity rooted in divinity. As created beings formed in the image and likeness of God, we inherently possess a divine nature. John said it clearly in his Gospel: "And of His fullness we have all received" (John 1:16). You can't contain the fullness of Jesus, the very Spirit of God, without measure, without equating that to divinity.

AWAKENING TO DIVINE IDENTITY

Paul unpacks this truth in Ephesians Chapter 1. He resolutely settles the divine identity of the Ephesian Christians, reminding them that they are absolutely complete in Christ. Our wholeness is found in the One who Himself is the fullness of the Triune God in bodily form. As we explore Ephesians, we'll firmly root ourselves in understanding that we originate from divinity and awakening to what that fully means as beloved sons.

As we explore Paul's letter to the Ephesians, I don't merely want to fill your head with knowledge. Building good theology is important, but that wasn't Paul's end goal here. More than crafting an air-tight belief system, Paul sought to impart revelation that transforms.

I imagine him grabbing the Ephesians by the shoulders, shaking them awake to the truth of their identity. His words carry an urgency — a desire to empower them to live here in this world as Jesus lives now. Theoretical principles matter little if we don't apply them. Paul wanted these truths to shake loose any lingering lies, rouse their spirits, and inspire a present-tense embodiment of Christ's likeness.

He wasn't penning a systematic theology textbook full of intellectual ideas to comprehend. He wrote to catalyze a shift, unveiling beliefs and blessings that change everything when genuinely embraced. I pray we recapture that sense of expectation as we walk through this letter together. More than increased knowledge, may these words resonate within us, realigning our perspectives and perceptions to see as Christ sees.

Let's approach this as a divine invitation to live abundantly awakened, not merely informed.

A LIFE OF ABUNDANCE

Paul tells us we've already been blessed with every spiritual blessing, past tense, done! But what does that really mean — "spiritual blessings"?

Everything we see in the physical world originated in unseen spiritual realms. God spoke creation into existence — the visible emerging from the invisible spirit realm. So when Paul describes blessings in the spiritual arena, he's pointing to the same creative power that transforms unseen potential into tangible reality.

When Paul says, "You have been blessed with every spiritual blessing," he's taking you into that unseen realm and saying, "Look, in this unseen realm is everything that you'll ever need for anything in life, any situation, any problem, any dilemma that arises, there's a blessing in the spirit, even though you can't see it. It's within you." I'm glimpsing this truth more and more in my own life and it's beginning to take shape and manifest visibly.

Paul is unveiling a life without lack for them *and us,* where everything we need has already been provided and deposited in us.

Let's continue in Ephesians Chapter 1...

DISCOVERING OUR INEXHAUSTIBLE INHERITANCE

Verse 11: "In Him also we have obtained an inheritance."

In the last chapter, we explored four foundational truths that shape our identity:

- We have been blessed with every spiritual blessing in heavenly realms
- We were securely placed in Christ before the very foundation of the world
- We were predestined as sons
- We are fully redeemed

Now, in verse 11, we encounter yet another facet of our identity: the presence of an inheritance.

This inheritance is an integral part of your identity and is truly limitless. Its resources are inexhaustible, ensuring that you can never deplete it. This inheritance surpasses even your most extravagant dreams and aspirations; and God has directly deposited into your account.

> Let's explore a thought: When does one truly benefit from an inheritance? Is it something to be appreciated after we die, or is it meant to be enjoyed during our lifetime?

If you've ever been fortunate enough to receive an inheritance, you'll likely agree that the person who left it to you intended for it to enhance your life here and now. They wanted to offer you something that could bring joy and fulfillment here and now. It's not reserved for the afterlife but is meant for us to embrace and experience in the present. It speaks to a life of abundance, a way of living that reflects the fullness and rich-ness of the kingdom here on Earth.

You may be surprised to discover that death is an elevated awareness of a dimension beyond your current understanding. In this transition, you might encounter an even greater capacity to access this inheritance, one that exceeds your wildest expectations. Could this inheritance be designed for eternal enjoyment, with the depths of His will forever beyond our complete understanding?

The inheritance He has given you is the working out of His will in your life. It's a profound truth that His desires for us surpass our own, always steering us toward something greater and more fulfilling. Embracing this can be transformative. When you finally let go of your plans, releasing your tight grip on your personal aspirations, you'll discover that His plan for you is infinitely more satisfying. This realization doesn't come instantly; it's a journey. Over time, you'll see that what He wants for you is far richer, deeper, and more rewarding than anything you could have envisioned for yourself.

Even Paul needed time to grasp this profound truth.

In 2 Corinthians 12:7-10, we encounter Paul facing a personal struggle, described as a 'thorn in the flesh.' I believe this struggle is linked to his conflicts with the Judaizers, a group advocating for traditional Jewish practices in the early Christian community. However, the true nature of Paul's 'thorn' remains a subject of speculation. In his quest for relief, Paul fervently appealed to the Lord three times, crying out, "Lord, please remove this burden from me." Yet, the response he received was unwavering: "My grace is sufficient for you."

In other words, God is assuring Paul the will that He has for him is better than what Paul thinks should be removed to enjoy life more fully. Embracing this truth, Paul acknowledged, "Most gladly, therefore, will I boast in my weaknesses because it is in my weakness that God's strength is made perfect."

JOINT HEIRS WITH CHRIST

This inheritance isn't just a tiny, designated portion but is measured by the same vastness as Jesus' inheritance. Simply put, what the Father has given to Jesus, He has given you. Every blessing, revelation, and insight that is Jesus' also belongs to you. We are joint heirs with Christ. This means an equal share in the divine legacy. We share it together, equally, in the fullness of its glory.

From the beginning, You were intricately fashioned to be a complete reflection, model, and walk as the first Son, Jesus. In His wisdom, the Father has equipped you with all that the Son possesses, ensuring you are fully capable of embodying this role.

Romans Chapter 8, verse 29 beautifully states: "For whom He foreknew, He also predestined." This means that every individual God knew would ever exist on this planet was predestined to be transformed into the likeness of His first Son, Jesus. As a result, every person on this earth is an heir to the same divine legacy, sharing equally in the inheritance that Jesus receives. This realization dispels any notion of hierarchy; in God's eyes, no one is more or less favored. Understanding this, we should view one another not as superior or inferior but equally blessed with God's grace and gifts. This understanding should shape how we interact with one another, creating a sense of unity and mutual respect as we *all* share the same measure of divine blessing.

You have been pre designed and engineered in the very likeness of Jesus, the exemplar par excellence. As you look at the life of Jesus — the prototype, the exemplar, the original pattern, the firstborn — you discover what your life is to look like.

The verse from 1 John 4:17, 'As He is, so are we in this world,' might seem mysterious. Let me help make it clearer. What happened in Jesus' life should be happening in ours — and it is, perhaps, more than you realize. You are living out this truth increasingly with each passing year. Compared to last year, two years ago, or even five years ago, your understanding and embodiment of this truth have significantly deepened.

DESIGNED WITH A PURPOSE

The Father created you with a specific purpose in Christ, one that is meant to bring you the utmost joy and happiness. This aligns with how you were designed; His purpose and plan for

your life are the very things that will bring you the most fulfillment and contentment. It's often said that finding and
excelling in what we love leads to a fulfilling life. I wish I had
understood this earlier in life; it would have significantly influenced my life choices.

Many people spend much of their lives not fully realizing that
God knows what is best for us and that He was aware of us
even before our birth. Ephesians 1:4 offers a remarkable insight
into this, and it's echoed in the words spoken to Jeremiah. I
hope that what God revealed to Jeremiah becomes a revelation
for all of us as well.

Jeremiah 1:4 opens with a powerful statement: "Then the word
of the Lord came to me, saying..." When the word of the Lord
speaks to you, as it did to Jeremiah, it speaks directly to your
unique purpose, individual design, and the specific plan God
has for you. This revelation can be incredibly liberating and
elevates your understanding of life. For me, it instilled a deep
assurance that what I was doing was right for my life and that I
needed to simply get better at it.

This is what God spoke to Jeremiah about his life in verse 5:
"Before I formed you in the womb I knew you." This is remarkably similar to Ephesians 1:4. God shaped and knew us even
before birth. He sanctified us, setting us apart. Doesn't this

align with Ephesians 1, where He predestined us as sons before the foundation of the world? He said to Jeremiah, "I sanctified you, separated you for a purpose, and I ordained you to be a prophet to the nations."

What gave Jeremiah the deepest joy was living out the purpose the Father had crafted for him from the start. This is a powerful and inspiring truth. If you're uncertain about what God has designed you for, reflect on what brings you the most happiness. Pursue whatever fills you with joy. As a loving Father, God does not take pleasure in seeing you involved in tasks that feel burdensome or joyless. He desires for you to find genuine happiness and fulfillment in what you do.

Discover that passion that lights your fire! Age is not a barrier in this pursuit. Even if you're retired, you now have the time to explore what truly brings you joy. Whatever you enjoy, find a way to align it with advancing the Kingdom of God. The nature of your interest doesn't matter because God is right in the midst of whatever you do. He is always with you, never leaving or forsaking you.

Therefore, embrace whatever sparks your joy, recognizing that God instilled that passion in you. Pursue it with all your heart and aim for excellence. Don't hold back, whether it's setting off on a motorhome journey across the United States or exploring any other interest. In each place you visit, let your light shine brightly. God will open doors and create opportunities for you, no matter where you are.

GOD'S SEAL OF OWNERSHIP: SAFEGUARDED IN CHRIST

Let's continue with Ephesians...

Verse 13: "In Him you also *trusted,* after you heard the word of truth, the gospel of your salvation; in whom also, having believed, you were sealed with the Holy Spirit of promise."

He has securely embedded that inheritance within your life. Believing means responding to this gospel of your salvation. You are forgiven and made whole, and when you respond to this truth, there comes a knowing that you know the Father has sealed you, and you effortlessly remain steadfast in this state of grace.

Verse 14: "...Who is the guarantee of our inheritance until the redemption of the purchased possession, to the praise of His glory."

The blessing that Paul is building into their identity, *and ours,* that we've been sealed by the Holy Spirit. This seal guarantees that all of God's plans for us are secure and won't be lost.

This reminds me of my grandmother, Grandma Sass, and her method of preserving strawberry jam. She would use Ball Mason jars to store her homemade jam. After filling the jars, she sealed them with wax to keep them fresh. Then, she would store these jars in what she fondly called 'the cellar' — not a typical basement, but a dug-out area with stone walls and shelves. Stored in the cellar and sealed with wax, the strawberry jam was kept fresh, ready to enjoy whenever she wished.

God has sealed you, and the seal He has placed upon you is the Holy Spirit, which safeguards you like it did my grandma's strawberry jam. Nothing could get into that strawberry jam once it was sealed with that wax seal. It was preserved and protected. Once He sealed you with the Holy Spirit, there was nothing that was going to change you. (Sealed is very important; it's one of the things that helps us in our identity to know that who we are never changes — You are complete and whole in Christ and always will be.)

David recognized this truth in Psalm 24:1 when he proclaimed that the entire world and all its inhabitants belong to the Lord, who has sealed all of us. God has never relinquished ownership or possession of anything He has created. Can you imagine, even in your wildest imagination, the Father creating something only to let it become the devil's property? Absolutely not. That's absurd! He has sealed us with the Holy Spirit, and this seal is airtight, unbreakable by anyone but Him, and He won't break it until He redeems the purchased possession, which is you.

In the past, kings possessed rings with their personal seals, and when they sent a letter, they would impress their signet ring into hot wax, creating the king's seal. Similarly, God has taken and set His seal upon you. This seal serves as a mark of authenticity, confirming that you are genuine, and unmistakably signifies that you truly belong to Him. Apart from anything you do or don't do, you are irrevocably His!

PAUL'S HEARTFELT ENCOURAGEMENT AND PRAYERS

In verse 15, Paul takes a moment to offer words of encouragement. While this may not be the central theme of his message, it carries significant importance.

Verses 15-16: "Therefore I also, after I heard of your faith in the Lord Jesus and your love for all the saints, do not cease to give thanks for you, making mention of you in my prayers."

In these words, Paul expresses his heartfelt gratitude and encouragement to the recipients of his letter. I want to extend the same sentiment to all of you who tune in to my broadcasts and read my books. Your unwavering love and devotion to the Lord and your personal journeys are truly inspirational. Sometimes, when I have had the privilege of meeting some of you in person during conferences or events, it fills me with great joy. What's truly remarkable is that when we meet, it feels like I've known you my entire life. We feel like family!

In verse 15, Paul deliberately pauses, having shared heavy revelations with them. He takes a breath, not because he wants to hold back but because he's mindful not to overwhelm his audience. His sincere desire is to impart as much wisdom as possible. However, he takes this moment to allow them to catch their breath and prevent their heads from spinning as they absorb all he has shared.

Finally, he concludes the letter with heartfelt prayers for them. Like Paul, I pray that you won't just gain insight but also about have the wisdom and practical knowledge to apply it effectively in your life.

Verse 17-19: "That God may grant you not only a spirit of revelation but also a spirit of wisdom, the eyes of your understanding being enlightened; that you may know what is the hope of His calling, what are the riches of the glory of His inheritance in the saints, and what *is* the exceeding greatness of His power toward us who believe, according to the working of His mighty power."

In essence, he prays that what he imparts to them transcends mere words, that they may discern the spirit behind the words, recognize the presence of Christ in him, and embrace the same Christ residing within them.

In verse 20, Paul emphasizes the nature of the inheritance, praying that they recognize it as the very same power, the explosive *dunamis* power, that raised Jesus from the dead. He continues to pray that they grasp their elevated position in Christ, surpassing all principality, power, might, dominion, and every name that exists. We are sealed in Christ in that exalted place.

WE ARE HIS BODY: MANIFESTING HIS FULLNESS

In verses 22 and 23, Paul unveils another crucial aspect of our identity, which I absolutely love.

Verses 22 and 23: "And He put all *things* under His feet, and gave Him *to be* head over all *things* to the church, which is His body, the fullness of Him who fills all in all."

Paul is constructing a deep understanding of their identity — *and ours* — as the body of Christ. Together, we constitute His body, with Him as the head. As the body, we represent the fullness of Christ, with all things placed under our feet. You and I are the full embodiment of Christ. You are the human you, and Christ is the eternal spirit in you. You are His fullness because He fills all and is in all.

Our identity finds its roots in divinity, and we've uncovered the limitless inheritance that accompanies it. We've found that this inheritance isn't a remote promise; rather, it's a current reality — a life of abundance meant to be embraced in the present. We must wholeheartedly embrace the truth that we are co-heirs with Christ, equally sharing in the divine inheritance.

Just as Paul shook the Ephesians awake to their identity, let us remain expectant, knowing that these words have the power to realign our lives and inspire us to live abundantly awakened, not merely informed.

Embrace the fullness of your identity in Christ, for you are the embodiment of divinity, filled with the eternal spirit of Christ.

3
UNVEILING ETERNAL TRUTHS

The pure gospel carries an irresistible quality — once truly grasped, it elicits transformation. This dynamic shines through Ephesians Chapter 2, where Paul dismantles restrictive mindsets to unveil breathtaking freedom.

He leaves no stone unturned in showcasing the Father's all-encompassing heart. Embedded within Ephesians lies a vast revelation, an eye-opening awakening awaiting all creation. While the book of Romans systematically develops theological doctrine, Ephesians stirs sheer wonder at the implications of our identity. You can't help but do a happy dance as you read it.

Read it as if you are reading it for the very first time. Remove any filters of religious assumption and read it with fresh eyes, allowing your spirit to embrace radical realities typically diluted by rigid theology. Don't read it as a scholar but rather as the son or daughter of God that you are. What you find may spur spontaneous celebration!

Let the Holy Spirit guide your study, unlocking spiritual dynamics you've yet to experience fully. Catch a glimpse of the Father's goodness as you soak in Paul's revelation of your identity in Christ.

Let's dive in and explore these first 10 verses of Ephesians Chapter 2...

Verses 1-10: "And you, *He made alive,* who were dead in trespasses and sins, in which you once walked according to the course of this world, according to the prince of the power of the air, the spirit who now works in the sons of disobedience, among whom also we all once conducted ourselves in the lusts of our flesh, fulfilling the desires of the flesh and of the mind, and were by nature children of wrath, just as the others. But God, who is rich in mercy, because of His great love with which He loved us, even when we were dead in trespasses, made us alive together with Christ (by grace you have been saved), and raised *us* up together, and made *us sit* together in the heavenly *places* in Christ Jesus, that in the ages to come He might show the exceeding riches of His grace in *His* kindness toward us in Christ Jesus. For by grace, you have been saved through faith, and that not of yourselves; *it is* the gift of God, not of works, lest anyone should boast. For we are His workmanship, created in Christ Jesus for good works, which God prepared beforehand that we should walk in them."

MADE ALIVE IN CHRIST: ALL GOD'S DOING

Notice how Paul opens — with the simple yet profound declaration that God 'He made us alive!' What a glorious gospel wrapped in just 4 words!

Before mentioning anything about sin or death, verse 1 anchors us in the security of God's grace declaring that He made us alive in Christ. It establishes grace as the starting line, not some position we reach after effort. Out of the gates, we see how good God is.

The first 10 verses of Ephesians Chapter 2 might be the most clear passage in scripture laying out the gospel. In quick succession, Paul unveils the Father's plan, motivation, vision, methodology, and lavish kindness which will take all of eternity to unpack fully.

Verse 4 explains the "why" behind God's nature and actions. Why does God do what He does? —because of His unconditional love for humanity. His mercy toward us flows out of His love. According to Strong's concordance, mercy is kindness toward those afflicted with the desire to relieve them.

Here's the Don Keathley definition of mercy: God looks upon anyone in a mess and says, "I'm going to get you out of this." He promises those with problems, "I'll solve them for you if you'll let Me." His love, demonstrated through mercy, solves every dilemma.

He's rich in mercy. He doesn't have shallow pockets when it comes to mercy. The psalmist tells us His mercies are new everyday.

" Consider this: If everything God does flows out of love, and His mercy demonstrates love rather than the cold, impersonal dictates of the law, how could He possibly leave anyone in eternal separation?

That would require limiting love's reach and denying mercy's innate drive to alleviate suffering. Instead, we must reconceive Him as complete Love unleashing waves of grace and mercy upon all creation, motivated by a depth of care beyond measure.

Verse 4, therefore, anchors the passage in the foundation of love. It sets the tone for correctly interpreting all that follows regarding God's intervention to restore humankind to our intended design. We must learn to read these first 10 verses through the lens of His rich mercy and love, overcoming all to achieve His divine purpose in our lives.

Verse 4 spotlights God's motivation — a love so immense it compels mercy. Then, verse 5 diagnoses humanity's core problem: We were dead in trespasses. But instantly, *while in that condition*, God made us alive together with Christ! No prerequisites were given, and there were no hoops to jump through first. No repentance required! It was out of sheer grace, in pure love, He made us alive.

This "deadness" means losing touch with identity and purpose, being destitute of life, or being inoperative. We wandered, entangled by lies about who we were and deviating from God's plans and purposes. But even then, in the darkest unconsciousness, Life Himself rushed in to restore us to the Truth, to make us alive together with Christ.

This concept aligns with what Paul stresses in Colossians 1. There, he describes us as alienated in our minds by wicked works. But *while in that condition*, verses 21 and 22 declare that God has reconciled us in the body of Jesus' flesh through death, to present you holy, and blameless, and above reproach in His sight. Dead in our trespasses, and alienated in our minds by wicked works are saying the same thing.

Adam took us off track, deviating from his course. The deviation was in his mind. He thought God was angry and separated from him. But that was untrue. Adam's distorted thinking about God caused him to become inoperative and ineffective, blocking the flow of Life — or, as Ephesians 2:5 says, to become dead in his trespasses. However, grace set us back on course and made us alive together with Christ, reconciling us once again. Though we forgot our identity, God never forgot us.

Grace is a one-way act of love that requires no response or contribution from the recipient. It is God's gift to us. Grace saved us. The word 'saved' does not mean a ticket to heaven; religion has completely misinterpreted the meaning of the word and misused it. Nowhere in the word 'saved' (*sozo* in Greek) does it refer to our eternal destination; it is about soundness, wholeness, wellness, and restoration to be experienced *now in this life*.

Even if we only understood verses 4 and 5 and knew He showed mercy to us because of His great love, catching hold of us when we went off track, setting us back on track by grace, being restored, made whole, made well, and kept safe from danger, it would be enough for us. That's the gospel! Yet, then he goes on in verse 6 to tell us that God raised us up together and made us sit together in the heavenly places in Christ. This is powerful stuff!

Verse 7: "That in the ages to come He might show the exceeding riches of His grace in His kindness toward us in Christ Jesus."

God's vision for eternity shows that His love and mercy never end, but the love and mercy continue to flow for us. This thing continues to unfold and unwind. Paul is talking about a love that never falters or fades. It is liberating to realize that God has no intention of ever withdrawing His love, mercy, and kindness. The relationship remains in motion, endless revelation of goodness awaiting us. Our experience of it has only scratched the surface thus far.

Verses 4-6 emphasize that it's all God's work. Through His immense love and mercy, He makes us alive, saves us by grace, and raises us up with Christ in heavenly places.

But there must be something we need to add to this, right? Perhaps in verses 8-10, Paul will to turn to us and tell us what we must do, right? After all, that's what we've been taught. But no, Paul doesn't turn to our role in this; instead, he reaffirms that it's never been about our efforts or actions. The focus remains on God's grace and initiative.

Verses 8-9: "For by grace you have been saved through faith, and that not of yourselves; *it is* the gift of God, not of works, lest anyone should boast."

Grace and faith are both from God. For years, I understood that verse as meaning that we were saved by His grace, but it came about by my faith. Verses 8 and 9 confront such presumptions. Any idea that we partnered even partially in procuring grace or mustering faith proves blatantly false. God gives grace and faith from start to finish.

And verse 10 definitively excludes any work on our part as well!

Verse 10: "For we are His workmanship, created in Christ Jesus for good works, which God prepared beforehand that we should walk in them."

Nothing dilutes pure grace like injecting personal effort. These verses crush all boasting of self-effort, giving no margin for patting ourselves on the back. That deflates religious ego. Surrendering control of earning a small foothold into God's kingdom leaves us feeling helpless.

What is a 'work'? A work is an effort, deed, or undertaking — even mentally, that we think we can bring to the table and contribute to what God says He has already done. God took our works out of the equation. There is to be no boasting about what we have done, what we haven't done, or what we must do. No looking down our nose at others who haven't performed the correct set of tasks to be saved — praying the prayer, confessing sin, making a decision for Christ, etc. God excludes all such works.

> Our salvation was all His doing. We all stand accepted, loved, and complete in His embrace with no edge over anyone else.

Religion told us we were created in Adam, but the truth is we were created in Christ. Paul is clear about that. Verse 10 says that we are His workmanship created in Christ Jesus.

Why is that important? Because it anchors our security. Paul is saying there was never a time when we were not in Christ.

I don't care what your church told you or your denomination hammered into you. If you were created in Christ Jesus, how could there ever be a time that you were not in Him? Created in Christ is an all-inclusive statement — *all* humanity was created in Christ. We can no longer label people as being in Christ or not in Christ. *All* were created in Christ.

God takes pride in His workmanship. He created all in Christ, stood back, looked at His creation, and said, "Very good!" Do you see the magnitude of that? His opinion of you is always "Very good!" You were a son and daughter of God; you were in Christ before becoming a Christian.

You won't find any verse in Ephesians Chapter 2 that is not about God's goodness and grace. These verses do not indicate anyone is lost. Our life, *including our future eternal destination*, is not in question. God has secured it.

But Don, if that's true, why aren't more people aware of the security of their identity in Christ?

MOST HAVE NEVER HEARD THE GOSPEL OF GRACE

Most people have not heard the Gospel of Jesus Christ, the Gospel of Grace. They've heard a religious message and rejected that, not Christ Himself. The religious gospel declares our origin in Adam. The true Gospel reveals we were created in Christ! So what happened to obscure this truth?

The first man, Adam, bought into the lie that he was not like God and, therefore, needed to do something to become like God. Man died in his awareness that he was one with the Triune God. Jesus came and conquered death in our awareness that had put a veil over our eyes, concealing the identity of who we always were — the image and likeness of God.

In Genesis 2:7, God breathed life into man's nostrils, giving him eternal life from the start. Just as we breathe air every day, His life within us never stops. God's act wasn't a one-time event; it was a continuous infusion of eternal life. Like our natural breathing, His life in us remains, even if we're not always aware of it.

We were co-resurrected with Jesus in newness of life and brought out of the tomb. Ephesians 2:5 declares, "We were made alive together with Christ." Adam released a lie into the human race, a corruptible seed planted into the mind of humanity, and consequently, we all bought into the lie of separation. But this separation was in our minds. We never had a fallen nature. Our nature has always been the breath of life, God's eternal life.

Jesus planted an incorruptible seed in our minds, replacing the lie about who we thought we were. This lie should have stayed in the grave, but religion resurrected it, teaching for centuries that we were born spiritually dead and inherently evil and separated from God. It convinced us we were irredeemably sinful and doomed to be judged by an angry God, who would be repulsed by us and cast us into eternal punishment if we didn't act. That's not the Gospel!

Remember, the Gospel is not about wavering love or condemnation. It's about the unchanging love of God, who has not condemned us but has made us fully alive together with Christ, reconciling us to Himself. Scripture does not depict humanity as born independent or separate from the Creator. The feeling of separation from God is a product of our imagination, not a reality.

In Acts 17, Paul goes to Mars Hill and talks with people who haven't prayed the prayer; they weren't believers in God and hadn't confessed their sins. He says to them in verse 28, "For in

Him we live and move and have our being..." These were idol worshippers, pagans! These are those that religion has deemed "outside of the faith!"

Paul continues, "As also some of your own poets have said, 'For we are also His offspring." Do you see what Paul is saying there to these pre-believers? Adam's perceived sin and separation from God were lies. It was all in his mind. Was it God's perception? No. He has always seen us living in Him, moving in Him, and having our being in Him — not as a potential but as our reality!

Religion's basis for teaching separation comes down to one verse in Isaiah. Isaiah 59:2 says, "But your iniquities have separated you from your God; And your sins have hidden *His* face from you, So that He will not hear." Isaiah didn't say our sins separated God from us. God's never been separated from humanity. That's the lie religion told us, that our sins separated God from us because He can't look on sin. That's not what this verse says.

In our awareness and perception, we had a sense of separation from God. But even in that, He reconciled us. There has never been a moment, even in our worst moments, when God could not or would not look upon us. We are His! God has always seen us and known us.

But Don, Isaiah said, "And your sins have hidden His face from you so that He will not hear you."

There are two false assumptions in that verse, and those two false assumptions produce a false conclusion. The false assumptions are:

1. God can't look upon you because of your sins/
2. Because your sins separated Him from you, He also can't hear you.

Let me ask you a question: If those two assumptions are true, then how does a sinner ever have the ability to repent?

Yet that's what religion says — because of sin, God can't see us, hear us, and He is separated from us, yet our repentance can change that. How can one repent to an unseeing, unhearing God? Do you see the insanity in that? How does religion back that up?

WE WERE NEVER SEPARATED FROM GOD

In Romans Chapter 8, verses 38-39, Paul says that nothing can separate us from the love of God: "Neither death nor life, nor angels nor principalities nor powers, nor things present nor things to come, nor height nor depth, nor any other created thing, shall be able to separate us from the love of God which is in Christ Jesus our Lord." In Hebrews 10:17, the writer assures us that God has said He remembers our sins and iniquities no more.

Yet religion has people confessing sins and iniquities that God doesn't even remember. Sin never separated us from God.

> Here's the truth: Everything is part of the one I AM. There's no dualism here; there's no God over there and you over here. Paul said in Colossians that Christ is all and in all and that all things hold together in Him. There's only one life, one power, one spirit, one mind, and one Lord. Zero separation.

Romans 11:36 says, "For of Him and through Him and to Him *are* all things, to whom *be* glory forever. Amen."

John 1:1-5 says, "In the beginning was the Word, and the Word was with God, and the Word was God. He was in the beginning with God. All things were made through Him, and without Him nothing was made that was made. In Him was life, and the life was the light of men. And the light shines in the darkness, and the darkness did not comprehend it."

So, in Him was *all* life. No life was created without Him, and the light shines in darkness, and the darkness did not comprehend it. The word 'comprehend' means to overcome or absorb. The darkness could not overcome or absorb light — it shines in the darkness.

Then John said in verse 9, "That was the true light which gives light to every man coming into the world." So, the light of verse 4 is His life. There is one life and one light; it's all His, and it lights every man who comes into the world. There's no separation. The light is in us. All we need to do is flip the switch. You're already wired. The light in us simply unveils what already eternally exists within us. Just flip the switch and shine!

ALL ARE IN CHRIST

Let's look at Colossians...

Colossians 1:16-17 says, "For by Him all things were created that are in heaven and that are on earth, visible and invisible, whether thrones or dominions or principalities or powers. All things were created through Him and for Him. And He is before all things, and in Him all things consist."

Paul said that *all* consists in Him. No one can be outside of Him; it's impossible. He is the only I AM. All humanity exists in Him. And because of our union with Him, we are all He is and nothing He is not.

So, when we say *I am righteous, I am justified, I am holy*, it is coming from the position of being a partaker of the divine nature, of our oneness with Him. Take time to let that sink deep within you; let it take root. There is only one I AM, and you're in Him who is I AM... you are I am in the I AM. We have never been apart from Him. How can one be apart from the One who is omnipresent?

> This separation message has got to go. It's time to expose it for the lie that it is.

In Colossians 3:11, Paul says, "There is neither Greek nor Jew, circumcised nor uncircumcised, barbarian, Scythian, slave nor free, but Christ is all and in all." He didn't leave anyone out in this verse. It is all-inclusive. Christ is all and in *all*. Noone is outside of Him.

Paul did a masterful job of articulating that in Ephesians Chapter 2, verses 1 through 10. But in our blindness, we thought we were independent beings. We falsely assumed we were the captains of our own ship, the masters of our fate apart from Him. No, that's untrue. The Father has had you in His embrace from the beginning, from before you were a glimmer in your parent's eyes. He secured your identity; He placed you in Christ before time began. Your life has always been secure in Him!

Let Grace break through any lies you may have held on to and see yourself as you are — made alive with Him, saved, made whole, raised, and seated in heavenly places in Christ Jesus.

4

LIVING AS SPIRIT-LED
BELIEVERS

In Ephesians 2:11-22, Paul continues to unpack the profound implications of the Gospel, revealing the transformation it brings to our identity and relationships. He confronts the historical divide between Jews and Gentiles, showcasing how Christ's sacrificial love dismantles the barriers that once separated them. Through vivid imagery, Paul illustrates how all believers, regardless of background, are now united as one new humanity in Christ, with equal access to the Father through the Spirit.

As we explore this passage, we'll see how Paul's message transcends mere theological concepts, inviting us to embody these truths.

We'll discover practical ways to discern and follow the Spirit's leading moment by moment, learning to live as mature sons and daughters of God. The chapter then delves into the transformative journey from living out of the soul to living by the Spirit. It explores the global spiritual awakening on the horizon and the increasing Spirit-to-spirit communication and revelation that characterizes this new era. Prepare to stretch your understanding of what's possible and ignite your hunger for deeper spiritual experience.

So, let's dive in and uncover the rich treasures in Ephesians Chapter 2, allowing them to reshape our understanding of who we are and how we're called to live.

UNITED IN CHRIST: NO MORE 'US AND THEM'

Verses 11-12: "Therefore remember that you, once Gentiles in the flesh—who are called Uncircumcision by what is called the Circumcision made in the flesh by hands—that at that time you were without Christ, being aliens from the commonwealth of Israel and strangers from the covenants of promise, having no hope and without God in the world."

Paul is drawing a distinction between Jews and Gentiles. He doesn't paint a very positive picture — they were without Christ, aliens from the Commonwealth of Israel, strangers from the covenant, in the world without God and without hope!

> What he's driving at is this: We were never under
> the Old Covenant as Gentiles; we were never
> under the law.

He's not telling them, *or us,* that we are without Christ, without God, and hopeless prior to believing. He's saying that *according to the Old Covenant*, we didn't have any hope. As Gentiles, we were on the outside looking in. He continues in verse 13 and says, "But now in Christ, you who were once far off Gentiles, you're now brought near by the blood of Christ."

Verse 14-15: "For He Himself is our peace, who has made both one, and has broken down the middle wall of separation, having abolished in His flesh the enmity, *that is,* the law of commandments *contained* in ordinances, so as to create in Himself one new man *from* the two, *thus* making peace."

There is no separation anymore between Jew and Gentile, those in the Covenant and those out of the Covenant. He's saying that it has been dissolved; that covenant is no more. Paul emphatically tells us that in Christ's own body, He abolished in the flesh this division, this enmity, this separation that the law produced, and He created from the two, the Jew and the Gentile, one new man and made peace between the two.

Paul declares the former dividing wall between Jew and Gentile has been demolished in Christ! Through His sacrifice, Jesus has ushered us all into God's presence, eliminating any distinction between "us and them" or "insiders and outsiders" within God's covenant. Paul explains that in Christ's flesh, He not only abolished the separation created by the Law but also united Jew and Gentile into one new man, thereby establishing peace. All humanity stands equally before God in Christ, sharing the same divine intimacy and fellowship.

Verse 16-18: "And that He might reconcile them both to God in one body through the cross, thereby putting to death the enmity. And He came and preached peace to you who were afar off and to those who were near. For through Him we both have access by one Spirit to the Father."

Christ provides the only access to the Father for both Jew and Gentile alike. There is not one way for the Jews and a different way for Gentiles. All now approach God the same way — by the Spirit. The same Spirit living inside every believer enables intimacy with God, regardless of background. Jesus eliminated all barriers and opened access for everyone.

BUILDING THE HOUSEHOLD OF GOD: ONE NEW HUMANITY IN CHRIST

Verses 19-20: "Now, therefore, you are no longer strangers and foreigners, but fellow citizens with the saints and members of the household of God, having been built on the foundation of the apostles and prophets, Jesus Christ Himself being the chief *cornerstone*."

Paul uses an architectural metaphor to explain God's design of the church. I've heard people say that Jesus Christ is the foundation of the church. No. Jesus Christ is the *cornerstone* — the integral originating piece to which the entire structure aligns. The rest of the building takes shape based on the cornerstone's alignment. Meanwhile, New Testament apostles and prophets provide the foundation and the support structure that the church, the body of Christ, is built upon. Their revelations laid the ground-level understanding of the Gospel message.

Verse 21: "In whom the whole building, being fitted together, grows into a holy temple in the Lord."

Paul summarizes his architectural analogy — Jesus as the church's determinative cornerstone and the apostles and prophets providing the theological foundation. Upon this

Gospel groundwork, the corporate body of Christ dynamically takes shape as God's Spirit-filled earthly dwelling.

Verse 18 is the key verse, affirming that we gain access into the kingdom, into the heart of the Father, by one Spirit. He goes to great lengths to emphasize that there are no longer two separate groups of people; there's only one new humanity — the new man in Christ Jesus. No Jew has a privileged position, and no Gentile remains excluded as foreigners of the covenant. All have access to the Father. This is the heart of the Gospel message — access to God not based on ethnicity, status, or past, but by the Spirit.

EMBRACING PRESENT TRUTH: A CALL TO SPIRITUAL TRANSFIGURATION

Peter emphasizes this in 2 Peter 1:12, stating he will continue reminding believers of 'present truth' they have heard before. Repetition makes revelation stick — the more we hear, the more it becomes part of us. But what exactly is this 'present truth'? It's revelation that the Father is speaking to us right now that He wants us to focus on and embody in our daily lives. Peter is adamant about ensuring believers are not just aware but firmly rooted in what the Father is communicating.

But how does this 'present truth' manifest in our lives today? How do we ensure we're in sync with what the Father is currently emphasizing?

Consider the monumental shift happening in the world today — this isn't merely about reformation or transformation. It's about transfiguration. Remember the moment of transfiguration on the mountain when Jesus, in the presence of Peter, James, and John, was enveloped in divine light and glory? A glory that was always there yet unseen by their natural eyes until that transformative moment. This is a vivid picture of what's unfolding right now. The Father is intricately working through our circumstances, revelations, and relationships, guiding us through a spiritual transfiguration.

He is meticulously clearing our path of every tendency to live from the soul — those habits and reactions crafted by our minds, emotions, and wills based on what we see, hear, and feel. It's as if we've been living in a room lit only by a candle, and He's inviting us into the sunlight.

I'm passionate about helping you distinguish between the voice of your soul and the whisper of your spirit. It's about moving away from being swayed by external forces and sensory perceptions that have long shaped our existence. We've navigated life according to the soul's map, drawn by our thoughts and senses informed by the tangible world around us.

The Father is transforming us from living out of the soul—guided by our minds, wills, and sensory perceptions — to living by the Spirit, where moment-by-moment responsiveness to His prompting becomes our norm.

> Have you felt this shift? Can you sense the Father's hand guiding you from the familiar terrain of the soul into the uncharted territory of the spirit?

SPIRIT-TO-SPIRIT CONNECTION

The beauty of our journey with the Holy Spirit isn't in chasing distant goals or visions, but in embracing the vibrant, Spirit-to-spirit connection we have with the Holy Spirit — accessible right here, right now. Romans Chapter 8 opens our eyes to a stunning truth: being led by the Spirit of God marks us as His sons and daughters. Imagine that — our daily walk, whether sharing a meal, baking a cake for a neighbor, or spontaneously altering our plans, becomes a dance with the Divine. This isn't just an idea; it's our reality, the 'present truth' that's actively shaping how we live.

And Paul doesn't stop there. In Romans 8:15-16, he unveils the heart of our relationship with God. We're not bound by fear, living as if we were slaves. No, we've been embraced by the Spirit of adoption, allowing us to call out to God as 'Abba,

Father.' The Holy Spirit whispers to our hearts, confirming deep within us that we are God's beloved children.

So, what does this mean for us? It means our response to the Spirit's nudges isn't out of obligation or fear but out of the secure, cherished place of knowing we are His. Whether it's deciding to call a friend on a whim or taking a different route home, these aren't just random decisions — they're responses to a loving Father's guidance woven into the fabric of our daily lives.

The journey with the Spirit is not marked by a singular moment of realization but is a continuous unfolding of our identity in Christ, assuring us we are sons and daughters of God. Each moment of listening and responding to the Spirit's leading increases our confidence in our identity and our ability to hear and follow His leading, empowering us to live tuned in to our spirit.

Furthermore, Romans Chapter 8, verse 17 opens our eyes to an even more astonishing truth: As His children, we're not just part of God's family but also joint heirs with Christ. This means we share in Christ's inheritance, and through a Spirit-to-spirit connection, the Holy Spirit will lead us into the full experience of our inheritance with God.

Being joint heirs with Christ means our destiny transcends mere earthly existence; we are called to manifest as God's sons and daughters in such a way that His kingdom's reality becomes evident here on Earth. This divine manifestation propels us into a life where we lack nothing and have access to everything we need, reflecting the fullness of His kingdom.

The kingdom of God is not anchored in a specific location but resides within us — a spiritual realm where we experience the Spirit's leading. As we learn to discern 'present truth,' we discover a new way of living — one marked by moment-by-moment attentiveness to the Spirit's leading, secure in our identity as beloved sons and daughters. This posture empowers us to manifest God's kingdom wherever we are, not from striving but from rest, walking in the fullness of our inheritance in Christ.

In moments of uncertainty and searching for direction, we often look outside ourselves, seeking prophetic words or advice to find clarity and purpose. Yet, 1 John 2:20 reminds us of a remarkable truth: we are anointed by the Holy One, equipped with divine enablement that empowers us beyond our natural capacities. This anointing isn't just for extraordinary tasks; it guides us in everyday decisions and challenges, offering wisdom and strength that surpass our understanding. It's a tangible presence of God's empowerment, enabling us to navigate life with insight and assurance that comes from being in tune with His Spirit.

This divine enablement manifests in practical ways—whether it's making a crucial decision with unexpected peace, finding clarity amidst confusion, or stepping out in trust when the outcome is uncertain. The key is nurturing our relationship with the Holy Spirit, the source of this anointing. As we lean into His presence and listen for His guidance, we access the wisdom and courage needed for each moment. This isn't about possessing all knowledge but about having the right wisdom at the right time, transforming how we face life's uncertainties with confidence and peace.

MAKING SPACE TO HEAR GOD CLEARLY

Shifting from a soul-led life to a Spirit-to-spirit-led life simplifies everything. It means reducing clutter like too many books, excessive TV watching, overeating, and complex relationships that distract us from God. If you struggle to hear God, it may be time to examine your life for distractions. Think about what you're focusing on. Is it social media, the news, or something else causing stress? It might be necessary to limit these things to clear the noise and better hear God's voice.

Finding quiet time is essential for staying spiritually connected in our busy lives, filled with messages, calls, and emails. It's about managing the constant demands and avoiding diversions that distract us from our spiritual focus. Simplifying life isn't just about doing less; it's about making space to hear God more clearly.

Simplifying our lives, honing our spiritual sensitivity, and grounding ourselves in what God communicates to us today is essential because, as Paul highlights in Ephesians 1:9, a mystery has been unveiled to us. This revelation prompts us to ponder deeply: What is the Spirit saying to me now? What truth should take root in my life so deeply that I actually embody this word, living it out fully?

As Paul further explains in verse 10, the mystery is God's grand plan to unite all things in Christ — everything in heaven and on earth. This unity isn't about the rapture or the second coming but about a divine purpose unfolding through time, aiming to restore all creation to its original unity in Christ. It's a reminder that we were placed in Christ before the world began, but we've drifted from that spiritual truth into a more soul-driven existence.

God intends to realign all things back into harmony in Christ, and remarkably, He chooses to work through us to achieve this. It's not about the monumental acts we might dream of but the everyday interactions and the inherent qualities that make us unique. Your personality, location, job, and skills — all these aspects of who you are become tools in God's hands, drawing people and creation closer to Him.

Even if you feel ordinary or believe you haven't achieved much, God values you immensely as His instrument. Whether you're engaging with others in stores, at work, or in your community, God uses your presence and words to reveal His glory. Simply greeting someone could reflect God's love and draw them nearer to Him. We're called to embrace our individuality and live out our divine purpose, for through us, God seeks to unify all things into one place in Christ.

The revelation of our divine inheritance and the deep things of God has often been veiled to us, waiting for our spiritual maturity. In Galatians, we learn that the child-heir differs nothing from the servants, although he possesses everything yet accesses nothing until he matures. This concept of spiritual inheritance being held in "escrow," so to speak, waiting for us to mature, emphasizes a deep truth: *Maturity is necessary to fully grasp and utilize what God has prepared for us.*

In 1 Corinthians 2, we discover why our spiritual inheritance and the plans God has for us often remain unseen. In verse 9, Paul tells us, "Eye has not seen, nor ear heard, nor have entered into the heart of man the things which God has prepared for

those who love Him." This tells us that our natural senses —
what we see, hear, and even what we think — can't grasp the
fullness of what God intends for us. Our attempts to understand God's plans through these means fall short because His
preparations for us go beyond our natural comprehension.

But there's a beautiful revelation that follows. God has chosen
to reveal these mysteries to us through His Spirit. Verse 10
highlights, "But God has revealed *them* to us through His Spirit.
For the Spirit searches all things, yes, the deep things of God."
This is an invitation to dive deeper, beyond surface-level
understanding, into the vast depths of God's heart and plans.
The Spirit within us is the key to unlocking these mysteries,
providing insight into things unseen and unheard by our
natural faculties.

Paul continues in verse 11, emphasizing that just as no one
knows a person's thoughts except their own spirit, no one can
know God's thoughts except through the Spirit of God. We
haven't been given the spirit of the world but the Spirit from
God, enabling us to know — to truly know — the blessings
freely given to us by God. This knowledge isn't about intellectual understanding but a deep, spiritual revelation that transforms how we see our lives and our union with God. Through
the Holy Spirit, we're granted access to the deepest truths of
God, inviting us to explore and embrace the rich, spiritual
inheritance He has prepared for those who love Him.

God is actively working in our lives, clearing away distractions and barriers that prevent us from fully grasping His purpose for us. As highlighted in Galatians 4:1-2, this maturation process involves being under guidance — through "governors" and "tutors" appointed by God until we reach a point of spiritual maturity and readiness for what He has planned. Governors in this context are likened to those who set our pace, ensuring we neither rush ahead nor lag behind in our spiritual journey. Tutors, on the other hand, provide direct instruction, teaching us through the learning stages of our grace walk.

GROWING IN GRACE

The journey of spiritual growth often leads us to explore new voices and perspectives. I've gravitated away from the authors and speakers I initially leaned on. Now, I seek out those who continue to dive deeper, offering fresh revelations and understanding. This change in who I learn from highlights a key part of growing spiritually: We must keep moving and exploring, not remain stagnant.

Some teachers linger on a singular insight or theme without further exploration or expansion. While this may offer comfort to some, it can limit growth for those seeking deeper understanding. On the contrary, others are constantly growing, challenging both themselves and their followers with new interpretations and insights. These are the individuals I find myself drawn to now — those who are not content with where they are but are actively moving forward, pushing the boundaries of traditional understanding to lead us into richer, more profound territories of grace.

This dynamic approach to spiritual teaching encourages continuous learning and growth, allowing us to keep pace with the ever-expanding revelation of God's truth.

These governors and tutors are the fivefold ministry. These leaders, as outlined in Ephesians Chapter 4, verses 11 to 15, play a crucial role in our spiritual growth. This ministry consists of apostles, prophets, evangelists, pastors, and teachers, all gifted to the body of Christ not for personal gain or to build their own ministries but to guide us toward becoming fully mature in Christ.

> Their goal is singular: To help us reach the stature of the fullness of Christ, which requires the contribution of all five roles, not just one.

The journey with these spiritual leaders should ultimately lead to independence, where believers learn to seek God, understand His grace, and discover His truths on their own. A true leader in the fivefold ministry aims to empower and release believers to grow beyond the need for constant guidance, encouraging personal revelations and a deeper, direct relationship with God. This shift represents a move from centralized, personality-driven leadership towards a more grassroots, collective growth in grace, where every believer is valued and has a place in spreading the message of God's love and acceptance to the world.

Back in 2003, I felt like a pioneer in these teachings, isolated and without much support. It was a time when connections were scarce, and the sense of community we enjoy today seemed unimaginable. Now, we can connect globally, finding solidarity and shared understanding. This shift underlines a vital preparation by God, not just for me but for all who are drawn to this message. It's crucial to discern the intent behind the voices we heed. If someone is focused on building their own platform or ministry for self-gain, it's wise to step back. True guidance aligns with 'present truth' and aims to deepen our understanding of our direct relationship with God, as seen in 1 John 2:20 and 27. These verses remind us of the anointing we each possess, empowering us with knowledge and independence through the Holy Spirit, negating the sole reliance on human teachers.

Recognize and embrace your anointing, which equips you with a divine confidence to stand firm in your beliefs, even in isolation or misunderstanding. This doesn't mean shutting out all external inputs. I continue to learn from others, seeking out teachings that resonate and contribute to my growth. However, there's a balance to maintain; while open to learning, we must critically evaluate and integrate these insights according to God's direction for our lives. Ultimately, the responsibility for what we allow into our lives, what we listen to, and what influences us rests with us. It's our duty to discern, accept, and cultivate these inputs to align with God's vision for our role within the broader spiritual community. This accountability doesn't imply shutting out external voices or teachings; rather, it emphasizes the importance of being selective and intentional about them.

Like my grown daughters, who have their own families but still sometimes seek advice from their dad, being spiritually mature doesn't mean you stop seeking guidance or listening to others. My daughters make their own decisions, sometimes following my advice and sometimes not. Similarly, having your own spiritual understanding or platform doesn't mean shutting out all other voices. It's about reaching a point where you no longer need someone else to spoon-feed spiritual truths to you. You're mature enough to discern, choose, and feed yourself on your spiritual journey, yet open to guidance when you seek it.

Central to our spiritual journey is the ability to perceive in the spirit — to see and hear beyond the natural. Without this spiritual insight, navigating the path God sets before us would be like wandering without a map. Jesus promised that the Spirit of Truth would reveal things to come. His guidance might unfold step by step, showing us the way forward even when our spiritual vision is still developing, and the full picture isn't clear. The key is to respond to the Holy Spirit's leading, recognizing and moving with the internal stirrings and resonances that signal His direction.

In the kingdom, our roles as kings and priests serve distinct yet equally crucial functions. Kings are tasked with governing the kingdom's affairs, while priests stand before God on behalf of the people. Embracing our role as kings involves stepping into a place of authority, a concept that might push the boundaries of conventional understanding. It suggests a shift from operating primarily through faith to moving in authority, dominion, and power.

What do I mean by that? Looking at Jesus' ministry, we see He rarely, if ever, framed His actions as acts of faith. Instead, He exercised dominion, governed by an unshakeable authority and power. This perspective invites us into a deeper realization of our identity and calling. When we truly understand and accept the authority granted to us, we find ourselves in a position where faith, as we typically understand it, transforms into a knowing. This knowing — a deep, visceral conviction — becomes the foundation from which we operate, marking a transition into dominion. It's about being so aligned with

God's will and confident in His backing that our actions stem from certainty rather than hope. This is the earmark of true dominion in the kingdom.

A GLOBAL OUTBREAK OF LOVE

God's ultimate vision is for us to operate in both our priestly and kingly roles, leading to a world where the knowledge of the Lord is as pervasive as water covering the sea. This future, as envisioned in Hebrews 8:11, is one where everyone, from the least to the greatest, will possess an intimate knowledge of the Lord. Considering the current culture we live in, a world where this knowledge is universal is exciting and mind-blowing.

The recent experience with the coronavirus pandemic illustrates how quickly something can encompass the globe. Although the virus spread fear and was certainly not of God, it demonstrated the rapidity with which a message or phenomenon can reach a worldwide scale. This example, albeit negative, underscores the potential for something as positive and transformative as the love of God to spread just as swiftly and completely — becoming a global love outbreak! It's a reminder that God's plans can unfold rapidly, igniting a global awakening to His presence and love, fundamentally changing the spiritual landscape of our world. Don't think this has to take generations and generations. I don't buy into that. I sense that we're much closer to a global spiritual awakening than many realize — almost on its threshold. This isn't a distant dream, hundreds of years in the future. Instead, it's a reality unfolding right now, in our present day. It feels as though we're already experiencing the 'coming attractions' of a profound shift that's heading our way, indicating that significant changes are not just possible but imminent.

SPIRITUAL COMMUNICATION TRANSCENDING WORDS

God is establishing a people who can see, function, and experience unity in the Spirit. My hope for you is to develop an effortless ability to hear in the Spirit, preparing us for a future where communication transcends words, enabling us to connect spirit to spirit.

Imagine if our usual ways of connecting, like the Internet, were unavailable. In such scenarios, deep spiritual sensitivity becomes essential. It allows us to be fully present in the physical world while also deeply connected to the spiritual realm.

This advanced awareness and connection could be described as vibrating at a higher frequency. While we've referred to this in the past as 'going to the next level' or 'entering a higher dimension,' it essentially involves elevating our spiritual frequency. The Fruit of the Spirit —love, joy, peace, gentleness, goodness, patience, kindness, faithfulness, and self-control — amplifies this frequency, guiding us to 'the next house in the mansion.'

Jesus metaphorically described this as the many mansions, which are levels of consciousness or awareness and realms of existence.

As we increasingly embrace the spiritual realm, our communication will transform, becoming intuitive and word-less. This shift makes intermediaries like prayer chains or support calls unnecessary, as revelations will flow directly from person to person through a spiritual connection. Therefore, it's time to move beyond merely hoping and asking for what we need. We should recognize that God has already provided, and we possess what we require.

God is transitioning from acting sovereignly on Earth to working through His manifested sons and daughters — those deeply responsive to the Spirit's leading. Our spirits will resonate like a guitar string that exists both within us and within the Father. When He strums that string, it will vibrate within me, and the same vibration will be felt within you. This spiritual tuning allows us to discern who to pray for, who needs provision, and who requires assistance around the world, all through the spirit to spirit connection.

This spiritual sensitivity can manifest uniquely for each person. Some may receive divine insights through dreams, experi-encing revelations they've never had before. Others might find clarity through contemplation or meditation, and things begin rising from within their spirit, much like Paul's experiences described in 2 Corinthians 12, where he speaks of visions that transcend ordinary understanding. Similarly, in the Acts of the Apostles, Ananias received clear direction to assist Paul, and Peter received revelations about the inclusivity of God's kingdom, showing that divine guidance can come in many forms, including dreams, trances, and direct communication from the Spirit.

These biblical examples underline that as we grow closer to God and more attuned to the Spirit, we will walk in a new dimension of spiritual awareness, where God's prompts and guidance become clear and actionable in our lives. This new way of living in the Spirit opens up pathways for us to participate actively in God's work on Earth, each according to the unique manner in which we receive and interpret the Spirit's leading.

Why aren't these experiences common today? —because we lack the deep spiritual connection required. We need to simplify our lives and eliminate distractions. In Paul's time, there weren't the numerous mediums we have today like television, the Internet, social media, or radio. These modern distractions can disrupt our spiritual frequency and prevent us from experiencing such profound encounters described in 2 Corinthians 12, Acts 9, and Acts 10.

Jesus fully understood this, which is why He walked on water and performed miracles. I believe quantum physics offers insights into the mechanics of the kingdom, revealing how these phenomena operate. This understanding will transcend our current perception of space and time, aligning us with the *eternal now* of God's presence. There will come a day when time ceases to exist. It was created for our benefit, yet we've become enslaved to it. Our lives revolve around the ticking of the clock, but this wasn't the original intention. Time was meant to serve us, not the other way around.

As you embark on this journey of walking in the Spirit, you'll gradually shed the constraints of earthly limitations. Our task is to identify and remove the barriers that hinder our connection with God. It's through the Spirit that we access the Father, irrespective of our background. You already possess His Spirit within you. As you mature in your spiritual journey, you'll feel prompted to simplify your life, declutter distractions, and create space for quiet reflection and deep listening. This simplification is vital for anyone committed to walking in the Spirit, a path to which you, my friend, are undoubtedly called.

So, I encourage you to consider how you can streamline your life to better tune into the communication of the Holy Spirit with your spirit, hearing what the Father is speaking to you.

5
UNVEILING RESURRECTION
LIFE WITHIN

In transitioning to Chapter three of Ephesians, we encounter a significant statement from Paul: "For this reason I, Paul, the prisoner of Jesus Christ for you Gentiles." He is expressing his deep commitment to the Gentiles, who may not have encountered the gospel.

Many today, like the Gentiles in Paul's time, have yet to hear the message of grace. It's my belief that people haven't rejected Jesus Himself but rather the distorted messages they've received about Him, messages that stray far from Paul's true gospel.

THE UNVEILING OF THE MYSTERY: PAUL'S REVELATION

Verse 2: "If indeed you have heard of the dispensation of the grace of God which was given to me for you."

The term 'dispensation' in the NKJV is not the best translation for the Greek word *oikonomía*. Other translations use the word 'stewardship.' Stewardship implies oversight or management of a particular thing — in this case, grace.

Paul is saying that God has entrusted him with overseeing this message of unpolluted, pure, radical, hyper-grace for the Gentiles. And in verse 3 he tells us how this message of grace came to him.

Verse 3-4: "How that by revelation, He made known to me the mystery (as I have briefly written already, by which, when you read, you may understand my knowledge in the mystery of Christ)."

In verse 3, Paul describes how this revelation came to him as a mystery; however, he's unraveled it, and he's here to reveal it to all. So, what's the mystery?

Verse 4: "When you read, you may understand my insight into the mystery of Christ."

Paul makes it clear that the mystery revolves around Christ.

Verses 5-6: "Which in other ages was not made known to the sons of men, as it has now been revealed by the Spirit to His holy apostles and prophets. That the Gentiles should be fellow heirs, of the same body, and partakers of His promise in Christ through the gospel."

Every Gentile is a rightful co-heir, inheriting the same promises given to humanity in Christ. This inheritance is bestowed through the Gospel, which proclaims God's unconditional goodness and grace. The Gospel does not contain bad news.

Verse 7-10: "Of which I became a minister according to the gift of the grace of God given to me by the effective working of His power. To me, who am less than the least of all the saints, this grace was given, that I should preach among the Gentiles the unsearchable riches of Christ, and to make all see what *is* the fellowship of the mystery, which from the beginning of the ages has been hidden in God who created all things through Jesus Christ; to the intent that now the manifold wisdom of

God might be made known by the church to the principalities and powers in the heavenly *places.*"

PAUL'S TRANSFORMATION AND THE INCLUSION OF GENTILES

Paul was the most unlikely person to be carrying this message. Yet, he was chosen to unveil a mystery — to preach the incomprehensible richness found in Christ to the Gentiles. This mystery, which from the beginning was hidden in God, was finally revealed through Jesus Christ. What is the purpose behind this revelation of the mystery? —to make God's multifaceted wisdom known through the church, even to the Gentiles.

The idea that God would reveal His profound wisdom to the Gentiles, a group traditionally seen as have-nots, as outsiders of God's covenant, was deeply unsettling to the Jews. These Gentiles, often regarded as lacking in spiritual understanding, were now included in God's plans and granted access to His wisdom. This shift, which challenged the established norms and beliefs of the Jewish community, was shocking and scandalous!

Verses 11-13: "According to the eternal purpose which He accomplished in Christ Jesus our Lord, in whom we have boldness and access with confidence through faith in Him. in whom we have boldness and access with confidence through faith in Him. Therefore I ask that you do not lose heart at my tribulations for you, which is your glory."

As I dive into these 13 verses, I can't help but notice the massive transformation in Paul's thinking since that day on the road to Damascus. Consider his journey. He went from being the relentless persecutor of the early church and a radical terrorist to becoming the carrier of the Gospel. Paul's past was marked by destruction — he was a murderer who imprisoned people and tore families apart in his crusade against believers. He went to great lengths to eradicate those early believers from existence.

Yet, Jesus Himself chose him to carry the gospel, revealing the mystery of Gentiles' inclusion into God's family. Paul, once driven by a mission to exterminate believers, now champions the automatic inclusion of Gentiles in Christ.

Paul's audacity is truly remarkable! If I were to stand up in a church today and declare that I've unraveled a mystery never before seen by the church, I'd likely be accused of heresy! In our established understanding of doctrine, introducing new truths seems unthinkable. We often believe we have a monopoly on truth, and anything outside our established beliefs is deemed unorthodox. Yet, isn't it astonishing how beliefs of the early church, once considered orthodox, are now deemed heretical? However, there's a shift happening. The new normal is beginning to embrace the message of 'grace plus nothing' Paul introduced to the Gentiles.

Paul moved from deeply entrenched religious traditions to fully embracing the mind of Christ. Now, he's guiding the Ephesian Church to develop this same Christ-centered mindset. When Paul expressed his desire to "know Him," he means that he had to let go of everything he once believed in — all theology, all belief systems, all traditions — and start afresh from ground zero.

I remember undergoing the same paradigm shift in my personal life in 2003. I consciously decided to put aside everything I had learned — from university, Sunday school, and past teachings — and ask God to start fresh and show me truth.

EMBODYING THE MIND OF CHRIST

The initial 13 verses of Ephesians chapter 3 are about Paul leading the Ephesian believers into the mind of Christ. He urges them to put on the mind of Christ where authority develops; that's where we learn to rule and reign in grace. This is where dominion comes from.

This mindset isn't just about faith; it's about dominion. Jesus operated in dominion and authority. Just before His departure, He declared, "All authority has been given to me." He didn't say, "All *faith* has been given to me; therefore, take this faith and go." He said, "All **authority** has been given to me; therefore, I give you that same authority, and I want you to go and disciple the nations."

In the Chapter 1 of John's Gospel, we read that Jesus was the Word made flesh. We are reverse-engineering that process — we are the flesh becoming the Word. Our background, cultural influences, and ingrained habits have programmed us to follow our soul and fleshly desires rather than align with the Spirit and put on the mind of Christ. For many people, this concept is entirely foreign.

A crucial step in developing the mind of Christ involves transforming our approach to Scripture, realizing it is not merely a collection of concepts, principles, or moral guidelines. Its primary purpose is deep and personal: To be written on your heart by the Spirit of Truth and to become embodied within you. Scripture is meant to be internalized, shaping us into the image of Christ from the inside out.

This process does more than adjust our actions; it transforms our entire perception of reality, establishing a new way of seeing and interacting with the world. As we embody God's Word, we manifest His grace and forgiveness in ways far beyond our imagination. Our thoughts and behaviors start to change, reflecting Christ's significant life in us. Love and forgiveness become natural expressions of our being, and we experience an intimate closeness with the Father. The feeling of distance from God fades away as a deep sense of union permeates your being.

As you awaken to your unique expression of Christ, you experience His life within you. Paul's declaration in Galatians 2:20 becomes a reality: "...it is no longer I who live, but Christ lives in me." This awakening marks the beginning of a remarkable transformation. The baggage that has weighed you down for so long begins to vanish. The Spirit of God actively removes obstacles that hinder your spiritual progress, severing ties with anything that prevents the full embodiment of God's Word in your life. This divine intervention enables your very being to become a living expression of the Word, empowering you to live from the mind of Christ.

BREAKING FREE

It's time to shed two significant burdens from your life, and let's be clear — it won't be easy. You'll need to submit to the transformative work of the cross. But remember, this isn't about striving or doing more; it's about embracing the revelation of what He has already accomplished for you and *as you*.

1. **Unequally Yoked Relationships**

Unequally yoked relationships can be incredibly challenging. They are connections in which you find yourself spiritually and emotionally drained after interactions. Imagine each interaction like having jumper cables attached to your soul, draining your vitality and leaving you exhausted. For many, this isn't an occasional inconvenience rather, it's a never-ending recurring cycle.

Do you recognize friends or relatives who leave you feeling emotionally and spiritually depleted? Establishing boundaries with these individuals is essential for your spiritual growth. While you can still cherish these relationships, there needs to be a firm line they cannot cross — one where they no longer drain you emotionally or spiritually. Setting boundaries doesn't mean cutting ties or withholding love.

On the contrary, it means loving them in a way that respects your own well-being. When they attempt to 'attach the jumper cables' to you, it's time to gently but firmly remove them. Through your actions and your boundaries, you let them know that their previous methods no longer work and can no longer pull you down or drain your energy. This isn't about exclusion but creating healthier dynamics that allow you to thrive spiritually.

SPIRITUAL DISCERNMENT

Jesus understood the need to set boundaries with people who drain us. Not everyone around him had unlimited, direct access to Him emotionally or spiritually. In John Chapter 2 and verse 23, it says, "Now when Jesus was in Jerusalem at the Passover during the feast, many believed in His name when they saw the signs that which He did."

Many believed in Him when they saw the miraculous signs He performed. Yet, interestingly, according to verse 24, Jesus did not commit Himself to them, 'for He knew all men.' He understood their hearts and motives, recognizing that many were drawn not to Him but to what He could offer them.

This lesson from Jesus' life is crucial for us today. As you progress in your spiritual journey, you will experience changes that both you and others will notice. With this transformation comes the need to prioritize your time and energy thoughtfully. Like Jesus, who ministered at different levels of intimacy — engaging with the multitude, empowering the seventy, intimately teaching the twelve, and reserving His deepest emotional and spiritual connections for just three — there's wisdom in discerning the nature of our relationships.

Jesus' approach teaches us the importance of setting boundaries, not out of rejection or cruelty, but from a place of discernment. He understood that not everyone who seeks closeness does so with pure motives. Similarly, we must use discernment in our relationships, differentiating between those drawn to us for what we can give and those who seek genuine, Spirit-led connections. It's not about isolating ourselves but about encouraging healthy, meaningful relationships that contribute to our growth and well-being.

When spending quiet time with God, if your mind is crowded with concerns about others' problems and demands on you, take it as a warning sign. Such distractions might indicate that you're entangled in 'soulish connections' — relationships that drain rather than enrich your spiritual life. If certain people or groups consistently divert your focus from God's presence, interfering with your meditation or personal time with the Spirit, it's crucial to address this.

> The solution is clear: Sever those draining connections and, instead, channel your energy and resources towards relationships that rejuvenate you, contribute to your growth, and nourish your spirit.

Seek out and cherish reciprocal relationships where both parties benefit, growing together in their spiritual journey.

Jesus was a pro at this. He poured into Peter, James, and John because He knew they were ready to walk the same path He was on. We, too, should prioritize relationships that align with our spiritual direction and encourage mutual growth and support.

This principle extends beyond personal relationships to include the media we consume, our social media interactions, and our entertainment choices. If these elements deplete your spiritual energy, it's time for a reevaluation. Be discerning about what you allow into your life, ensuring it doesn't detract from the vision and truth you're planting in your subconscious, shaping your reality. Setting boundaries is not about isolation; it's about making wise choices to protect and enhance your spiritual well-being.

God is reprogramming us internally. As the Spirit of Truth shows you the soulish things that need to go and what needs to come in to feed your spirit, the old ways of thinking, the 'mind of the soul,' start to fade, and the 'mind of Spirit,' gets louder and stronger.

This transformation is not limited to our spiritual lives but extends to our physical well-being. The life of the Spirit within us sustains our bodies, so strengthening our spiritual life has a tangible effect on our physical health. As the inner man grows stronger in the Spirit, our physical body, the 'outward man,' starts to reflect this inner life, becoming more resilient to illness and better equipped for longevity.

RESURRECTION LIFE IN US

I desire for the same Spirit that raised Jesus from the dead to invigorate your mortal body. This indwelling Spirit breathes life into every cell, offering protection against sickness and enabling enduring health. As you strengthen this spirit life, you'll witness a remarkable synergy between your spiritual growth and physical health.

> Have you ever wondered how it feels to transition from seeing life as if through a foggy mirror to experiencing a clear, direct view?

In 1 Corinthians 13, known as the Love Chapter, Paul guides us toward this moment of awakening. It's not just about gaining clarity in understanding God's truths; it's about fully recognizing who we truly are in His eyes.

This shift is transformative. By grasping this fullness — seeing ourselves and knowing ourselves as we are fully known by God — we step into a life energized by the Holy Spirit. It's a life that mirrors the resurrection power that raised Jesus, a life where our spiritual understanding and physical well-being are intertwined. This deeper revelation from Paul invites us on a journey from soul-led to Spirit-led living, where our true identity is revealed, and our lives are empowered by the life of the Spirit within us.

This isn't about merely navigating through daily life; it's an invitation to view existence from a radically different perspective. The teachings of Jesus and Paul transcend theological discussions — it's a call to a deeper, Spirit-led way of living. There is much more to our existence as a new creation than we've understood. We are being asked to embrace the message that we're meant to live beyond the ordinary constraints of mortality — a message that challenges conventional understanding! But when you start diving into this message of grace, these are some of the revelations that the Spirit of Grace can give you to because you now understand how good God is.

In Romans Chapter 8, Paul lays a foundation that shifts our perspective on life and death. In verse 10, he says, "And if Christ is in you, the body is dead because of sin, but the Spirit is life because of righteousness." So, on one hand, the body died because of sin, but now the Spirit is giving life because you're righteous. Then, in verse 11, he says, "But if the Spirit of Him who raised Jesus from the dead dwells in you, He who raised Christ from the dead will also give life to your mortal bodies through His Spirit who dwells in you."

Paul isn't speaking metaphorically. This is a literal invitation to tap into a divine force that sustains and revitalizes our mortal selves. Resurrection life is a life that knows no death. That resurrection life always lived in Jesus. Resurrection life didn't enter Jesus when He was crucified — death never had power over Jesus, and death does not have power over you! Paul said that if the same Spirit that raised Jesus from the dead lives in you — and He does! — then He will give life to your mortal body.

UNLOCKING SPIRITUAL AUTHORITY

So why don't we see this happening more often? That's what we're going to explore. But first, let's look at what Jesus said in John 10:17-18: "Therefore My Father loves Me, because I lay down My life that I may take it again. No one takes it from Me, but I lay it down of Myself. I have power to lay it down, and I have power to take it again." Jesus had the power to lay down His life and take it up again. Scripture tells us that as He is, so are we in this world. Are you willing to embrace that fact?

As you read these words, can you let your imagination grasp the truth that nothing and no one can take your life from you? That if you were stoned or shot, you can take it back up again and lay it down only when you're ready to go? You have the authority to lay down your life when you're ready and have completed the journey you set out to walk. You can then say, "Father, I've done what I came to do. I'm ready to lay it down now." But until then, no one can take your life from you.

I realize that this might sound far-fetched, but I encourage you to let these truths sink in. Allow yourself to imagine the incredible power and authority you have in Christ. As these revelations take root in your heart, you'll begin to understand what realizing and living in the fullness of our spiritual heritage and destiny as a new creation looks like. It's a game-changer!

Look at what Jesus says at the end of verse 18, "This command I have received from my Father." What command did He receive from the Father? —The power to lay His life down and to take it up again! It's a deeper spiritual understanding that we enter into when we know that our job is done, we have run our race, and we choose to lay it down. It's also a profound spiritual awareness that we embrace when we say, "Nothing and no man can take my life from me. The power to lay it down belongs to me!"

The Don Keathley "translation" of Romans 11:36 says, "Everything comes from God, passes through God, and returns to God."

Are you confident in that? Once you know your origination you know your destination. The Holy Spirit's work within us is deeply personal. It focuses on aligning our thoughts with those of Christ, making room for His mindset to really take the lead in our lives. This transformative process involves discerning what should stay and what should go — relationships, habits, or media that distract us from our spiritual growth.

His work in us includes helping us shift to Christ's mind, fundamentally changing how we see the world. This involves challenging and removing false paradigms — those deeply ingrained ways of understanding reality shaped by our experiences, education, culture, and even our religious upbringing.

TRANSCENDING DEATH

Many of us, including myself, are on a journey to dislodge these distorted views. To truly embrace Christ's mind, we must identify and let go of these false paradigms. The first one was unequally yoked, and the second one is our understanding of life and death.

2. **Our current understanding of life and death**

The reason we haven't seen resurrection life evolve in us is that we still have a paradigm of death. Many believe in the inevitability of death without recognizing that death has no dominion over the mind of Christ.

What does embracing the truth of resurrection life look like in my life, especially when physical circumstances seem to contradict it? I've come to understand that the true source of my life is the Spirit within me — not the medication I take or the medical advice I follow. While I greatly respect the medical profession and participate in tests and treatments as recommended, I see these actions as methods to calm my mind. Deep down, I know it's the Spirit that raised Jesus from the dead dwelling in me; the Holy Spirit is giving me life. He isn't just a part of my life; He *is* my life.

It's time for us to challenge and move beyond the conventional understanding of death—as a process inevitably ending in disease, decay, and decline.

> What if we started to view death not as a final limitation imposed by our physical bodies but as a transition into a realm free from the desires of the flesh and the constraints of the mind?

Let's consider Paul's insights in Romans...

Romans 6:8 says, "Now if we died with Christ, we believe that we shall also live with Him." Do you believe you died and were crucified with Christ? Paul elaborates on this in Galatians 2:20 and 2 Corinthians 5:14, emphasizing that if Christ died for *all*, then *all* died. This isn't just a figure of speech; it's a spiritual reality that defines our identity as believers. His death was our death.

But what does it mean to live in this truth? In verse 9, Paul continues, asserting that just as Christ was raised from the dead, He dies no more; death has no dominion over Him. The same is true of you — you died with Christ, therefore death has no dominion over you. However, due to entrenched perspectives on death, this can be a challenging concept to grasp. It's time for us to sow new seeds of consciousness, affirming that our lives in Christ are not confined by worldly views of mortality.

TRANSFORMING OUR 'I AM' STATEMENTS

A key to this transformation is examining and revising our 'I am' statements. How often do we unconsciously limit ourselves with negative 'I am not' declarations? Aligning our self-affirmations with the divine 'I AM' enables us to live out the truth of our unity with Christ, surpassing the bounds of death itself.

> Let's actively declare, 'I am alive in Christ; death has no dominion over me.' Changing our 'I am' statements is more than optimistic thinking — it's a recognition of our newness of life and victory in Christ.

In our spiritual journey, transitioning from the 'mind of the soul' — influenced by worldly teachings and experiences — to the 'mind of Christ' is crucial yet challenging. This shift isn't what we've been conditioned to naturally embrace due to the countless influences from our upbringing, education, and social interactions. These external factors have instilled false paradigms that often obscure our spiritual vision.

I vividly recall the moment when my spiritual eyes were opened to the concept of grace. This revelation, like a powerful wave, fundamentally altered my understanding of God, and every time my eyes were opened wider there was another shift in my reality. Why? —because every step builds on the previous step.

Discovering grace changed everything for me. It led me to see God not just as the Creator, but as a loving Father. This new perspective transformed how I view God, shifting my understanding to unconditional love and endless mercy. Grace showed me God's true nature, which has made all the difference in how I live and love.

I've come to a place where I no longer see death as having power over us. But what keeps us bound to this limited way of thinking? —the false beliefs we've accepted without question. Our journey now is to uncover and challenge these beliefs. The main thing holding us back is our lack of vision, our inability to see beyond these old paradigms.

Your vision and revelations set the boundaries of your journey. To receive revelation, quiet your mind and focus on your deepest desires, whether starting a business, owning a home, or breaking free from past constraints. Begin to visualize that and let God begin to speak to you about it. Let those seeds drop into your subconscious.

Remember, 'as a man thinketh in his heart, so is he.' Your heart reflects what you truly think and believe. Your mind controls your thoughts, and your heart believes what you think. If you focus on fear, like worrying about an early death, your heart takes it as truth and it can shape your life. Be mindful of your thoughts, as they can become your reality.

The deeper the Holy Spirit works in us, the more we break free from chains, helping us see clearer. This cycle of seeing and freeing continues, leading to personal growth. Today, I'm shedding limitations I didn't even know I had a year ago, improving my teaching and understanding, and shifting my whole perspective from where I was even last year. My mind has shifted, changing my reality and attracting new experiences and people aligned with my path. Some old friends can't keep up with these changes. As my perspective expands, I change, leading to new ways of thinking that don't just change me — they entirely transfigure me.

Transfigure means to change completely, especially in appearance. We're cutting away our fears, anxieties, and burdens. It's hard to let go of harmful relationships and beliefs we've clung to for years. However, realizing that some doctrines, like eternal punishment, have wrongly influenced our view of God and others leads us to change. This shift in belief alters how we see the world, how we live, and how we treat people.

Abiding in His presence is now the focus of your life. It shapes your reality and introduces new ways of thinking. You're growing and changing, not stuck at the same level. As you let go of unequally yoked relationships and allow Holy Spirit to alter your understanding of life and death, your views shift from false to true. Your understanding deepens as you rise higher, like seeing more from the top of a skyscraper than a small house. This elevation of thought lets you see further.

You're experiencing an internal change, moving away from old religious ways with no desire to return. Everything feels different, like embarking on an adventure in an unfamiliar city, but through your Spirit-to-spirit connection, you're finding your way through this new landscape. You're adapting to this change, recognizing you're in a new phase of life.

God is stretching us more than ever before, making constant growth our new normal. Be ready for it. Your manifestation as a son is not out there someday in the future. You are manifesting now, and it's getting sharper and clearer.

Your outlook and relationships will change as you know yourself as God knows you. Just like Jesus and Paul, who kept their circles small and didn't open up to everyone, you'll find that not everyone will be close to you or have unlimited, direct access to your life. You'll find yourself being stretched in this new understanding of life and death. That's ok! Let yourself be led by the Holy Spirit's work within you.

The presence of the Spirit of Truth is powerful and will guide you correctly. Trust that you won't go wrong; He will steer you clear of mistakes. Find comfort in knowing that everything happening in your life is very good and divinely guided.

6

PRACTICING THE PRESENCE

At the heart of Ephesians Chapter 3, verses 14-21, lies a gem that's both challenging and incredibly rewarding. It's like stumbling upon a treasure map that doesn't just show you where the gold is but teaches you how to live so that every day feels like you've struck it rich. This isn't about skimming through a passage for the sake of it; it's about diving deep into a lifestyle change and being invited to understand what it means to truly live in the presence of God — not as a concept, but as a natural, tangible experience.

Paul kicks off this section with something that genuinely touches the heart. He's so moved by what he's learned about grace and God's love that he can't help but drop to his knees in awe. It's like he's saying, "Guys, this is it — living in God's presence is *everything*!" Paul's not just talking about feeling good on a Sunday morning; he's outlining a day-in, day-out kind of living that transforms how we see everything.

So, as we explore these verses together, let's keep it real and down-to-earth, focusing on how this deeply spiritual work happens inside us. It's about understanding that being in God's presence isn't about adding something extra to our lives; it's about recognizing that He lives in us and we live in Him. It's about an unbreakable, irrevocable union. Paul challenges us to notice what is going on within us and how that working takes place to bring us into that realm, into that dimension, into that place of consciousness or awareness where we live in the presence of God.

Let's dive in and see how Paul's message can take us from just reading words on a page to living out those words in our everyday lives.

OVERWHELMED BY GRACE

Verse 14: "For this reason, I bow my knees to the Father of our Lord Jesus Christ."

Paul starts with a decisive moment of realization. He's awestruck by the grace revealed through Jesus. It's a moment of clarity where everything else falls away, leaving only the pure Gospel of Grace. Paul is overwhelmed by grace, a feeling many of us can relate to when we first grasp the depth of truth and see ourselves through the eyes of the Father.

Paul is moved to the point of humility, physically bowing in reverence to acknowledge that this journey with God involves Jesus plus nothing else; it's pure grace. There's no addition we can make to enhance this spiritual walk — it's entirely the work of Jesus and the Father's love for us. Paul sets the scene by giving all credit and praise to God, highlighting that our part is simply to recognize and live within this grace-filled reality.

Verse 15: "From whom the whole family in heaven and earth is named."

That's a very inclusive scripture right there. Paul makes it clear: Everyone, everywhere, is included in the Father's family. No one is left out. God is the one Father of all humanity. He emphasizes the universal belongingness to God's family. He sets the stage to instill some key principles in the Ephesian church, guiding them into a life where experiencing the Father's presence becomes a daily expectation, a daily reality.

GOD'S HIGH OPINION OF US

Verse 16: That He would grant you, according to the riches of His glory, to be strengthened with might through His Spirit in the inner man."

Paul is reaching out to every one of us with a heartfelt invitation: He wants us to experience God's incredible power deep within, through the Holy Spirit. In laying out the groundwork, he shows us the initial steps towards living in a constant awareness of God's presence, where His presence isn't a visitation but a 24/7 reality. Paul's prayer for our strength isn't just about physical or emotional resilience, it's about being empowered by God's glorious power from within.

Paul prayed that God would grant us according to the riches of His glory. Glory is often seen as God's visible greatness. Yet, when you dive into the meaning of the word "glory" or *doxa* in Greek, there's an expounded meaning of the word that's fascinating. Paul discovered, and shares with us, that this glory isn't just about awe-inspiring majesty. It also reflects how God sees us — favorably, always in a positive light. This isn't a casual observation; it's a remarkable insight into how deeply God values us, always holding us in high regard. Through Paul's eyes, we're invited to see ourselves as the Father does, with a favor that's unwavering and full of might.

> Paul's message is simple yet transformative: God's view or opinion of us (His glory or *doxa*) — always favorable — is the foundation for our spiritual empowerment.

This favor is not just about being seen positively by God but about establishing a deep, Spirit-to-spirit connection that is the source of our true strength. It's a life flow that comes from His Spirit to our spirit. This connection transcends physical and emotional capacities, rooting our power in the very essence of our being — our spirit. Paul calls this our "inner man" or "spirit man," the central hub from where we can effortlessly listen, respond, and live in and from God's presence.

Verse 17: "That Christ may dwell in your hearts through faith; that you, being rooted and grounded in love."

As the Spirit strengthens your spirit, a deep change begins: The awareness of Christ's eternal Spirit, which filled Jesus, infuses your very being. This heightened awareness manifests in one form — love.

In verse 17, we learn that love is more than a feeling. It's the strongest force there is, sustaining us at our core. God's love is the greatest strength we can have in our lives.

RECOGNIZING THE FATHER'S PRESENCE WITHIN US

Paul is carefully building a foundation, step by step, towards a crucial revelation. He steers us toward a life where we're always aware of the Father's presence, not just now and then, but all the time. In this constant awareness, we discover our true strength, energy, and the essence of life.

> " Recognizing the Father's presence at all times isn't a choice; it's the very heart of our existence.

Embrace and allow the deep-reaching roots of God's love to permeate every aspect of your life. This isn't just any love; it's the *zoé life*, the divine life of God, a life characterized by an indestructible, eternal love. This very love is the wellspring of resurrection life. The powerful Spirit of Love, which raised Jesus from death, resides within us. Paul urges us to embrace this love, allowing it to permeate every part of us. It's an invitation to immerse ourselves in God's love, letting it rejuvenate us completely and leading us to a deeper understanding and experience of abundant life in God's presence.

WE ARE FILLED WITH THE FULLNESS OF GOD

Verses 18-19: "(that we)... may be able to comprehend with all the saints what *is* the width and length and depth and height — to know the love of Christ which passes knowledge; that you may be filled with all the fullness of God."

> Notice the transformation: Love becomes our foundation and anchor. As this love fills every part of us, it becomes our central operating system.

Paul's message begins with a call for us to be strengthened in our inner man. He introduces love as the essential element that roots and grounds us, suggesting that this love is deeply embedded within our beings. Paul's vision extends further, urging us to fully grasp the immense scope of this love — the height, depth, length, and breadth — encouraging an intimate understanding that transcends mere knowledge. This exploration reveals love's limitless nature; just as we think we've understood its extent, it expands even further, proving to be deeper, higher, and broader than we imagined.

This limitless, unconditional love doesn't just fill us; it enlarges our capacity to receive and share it, impacting how we live and manifest God's presence. Paul highlights the transformative potential of this love to continuously grow within us, leading to a remarkable conclusion: *We can be filled with the fullness of God.* This is mind-blowing! Did you ever imagine you had such potential? This idea challenges common perceptions, suggesting that instead of seeing God as a distant, somewhere in-the-sky God, we can recognize and embrace the *fullness* of His presence within us. Paul's heartfelt prayer was that we acknowledge that we are filled with *all the fullness* of God!

Being filled with God's fullness isn't like filling your tank with gasoline; you just keep pumping it in. When you're filled with God's fullness, you become a sharer in the divine nature itself. This filling is not a gradual increase, where you start with a little and gain more over time. Instead, you are fully immersed in it from the start. Our acknowledgment of this truth needs to grow, not the measure of God's presence within us. We have the fullness of God already in us.

> Paul suggests that whether in this life or the next, we're meant to fully recognize, accept, and live out God's fullness. This has always been God's plan for us.

Verse 20: "Now to him who is able to do exceedingly abundantly above all that we ask or think, according to the power that works in us."

The challenge is how much of this power we recognize and accept. Many seem stuck at a certain level of experiencing God's power, perhaps afraid to explore beyond what they already know. Paul urges us to break free from these self-imposed limits and boldly explore the immense depth of God's power. Don't let fear or hesitation hold you back; there's a world of strength and possibility waiting to be uncovered within you and turned loose.

Paul writes with the intent of inspired revelation, not merely to engage our intellect. His aim is for us to truly experience and understand the truth, the truth that brings freedom. It's not just about intellectual comprehension; it's about experiencing and living out that truth in our lives. It's not about grasping concepts and moving on to the next big idea. This isn't an intellectual pursuit where we simply understand and move on. It's not about grabbing hold of theories or steps with our minds.

When we truly experience Paul's revelation, it becomes the core of who we are. Paul desires a deep spiritual connection, where we are strengthened by God's Spirit within our inner selves. This is where we truly live and find the source of life. It's where we hear from God, where our actions originate; it's like the central switchboard of our existence.

We've reached a point in our growth where intellectual understanding alone isn't enough. We may have spent years in school, read countless books, and enjoyed expanding our minds, but mere knowledge falls short when it comes to spiritual life. If our spiritual understanding isn't translating into real-life experiences and manifestations, our intellectual pursuits are meaningless. It's no longer satisfying to simply grasp truths or crave new revelations. The essence lies in embodying our identity as manifested sons and daughters of God and helping others do the same.

I've realized that grasping intellectual concepts and theories isn't enough for me anymore. I want to go beyond that and start implementing those ideas. I want to be able to begin putting boots on the ground and demonstrating them. What does it truly mean to walk in the Spirit or live in the Spirit? It can't be explained; it must be experienced.

Let's recap verses 17, 18, and 19 to see what we are meant to experience.

Beginning with verses 17-18, "That Christ may dwell in your hearts through faith, being rooted and grounded in love, may be able to comprehend with all the saints what is the width, the length, the depth, the height, and to know the love of Christ which surpasses knowledge."

You're filling your spirit, your inner man with this. And this is what leads you into the deep water; this is what leads us into manifesting, this is the Love of Christ which surpasses knowledge. In essence, Paul is saying, "I want you to get this, and I want it to settle in so deep and so strong that it goes *beyond* your mind and *behind* your mind. I want it to saturate your inner man so that you may be filled — not in your head, but your inner man, your spirit man — that you might be filled with all the fullness of God."

Again, in verse 19, when Paul emphasizes knowing the *love of Christ which surpasses knowledge, that we may be filled with all the fullness of God*, he's talking about something we have to experience; we can't verbalize it, theorize it, or make an explanation of it that really sounds great. It must be lived out.

THE PAROUSIA: CHRIST'S ABIDING PRESENCE WITHIN

I hope you sensed Paul's heart and mine as we explored those verses. The Christ within me speaks to the Christ within you today; my spirit communicates with your spirit. We live in a period known as 'the *parousia*,' a Greek term that means the time of His presence; the strict definition is 'the Presence's arrival' or 'official visit.'

Let me relate this to our modern context. The church has often interpreted *parousia* as a fixed date for Christ's coming, creating fear and theological debates. However, it actually signifies a season of His arrival. I want you to understand that this season is *now*, and you can experience the fullness of His presence today.

Paul emphasized being filled with God's fullness, experiencing it, living it, and sharing it with others. Unfortunately, the church has become fixated on concepts like the rapture and the second coming. If that's your belief and where you stand in your spiritual journey, that's okay. However, the concept of the rapture and the second coming has often become a lens through which we interpret every event and aspect of life. It's led to a continuous state of hopeful anticipation, constantly living in a 'someday when He comes' mentality rather than living in the fullness of His presence *now*.

To be frank with you, I consider that to be a very soulish theology, rooted in human intellect rather than in Paul's teachings. It has limited our ability to experience the full presence of the Lord to a future time when He returns. Whether you believe in His return or not, I'm putting that aside for now. It's not the focus of my message in this book, although I have my own opinions on the matter. My main focus in this book on Ephesians is to convey that the season of Christ's presence, the *parousia*, can be experienced and enjoyed now. It doesn't have to be postponed until some future date.

Like most of you, I once read 1 John Chapter 3 and believed it was about the second coming. But let me share a different perspective on it with you.

The first part of verse 2 says, "Beloved, now we are the children of God." The emphasis here is on the present moment: '***now***, we are the sons, the children of God.' Continuing with verse 2 and 3: "And it has not yet been revealed what we shall be, but we know that when He is revealed, we shall be like Him, for we shall see Him as He is. And everyone who has this hope in Him purifies himself, just as He is pure."

> Seeing Him as He truly is will result in us manifesting our true identity in Him. We are not *becoming* pure. We are pure in Him. Our purity is a reflection of who He is within us.

Again, there was a time when I interpreted the second verse as referring to a future event, the second coming of Christ. If you hold that interpretation, it's okay, but I see it differently now. I believe John's message aligns with Paul's teachings. John is expressing that encountering Jesus and experiencing His love will bring about revelation. This revelation of love will transform us, conforming us into the image of the Son. Ultimately, we will manifest the One we behold.

This transformation is happening in the present moment. A manifested son of God requires a revelation of who Jesus is. Understanding that as Jesus is, so are we in this world is crucial. We are being brought into conformity with His image. The more we understand and see Jesus, the more we start to resemble Him. This isn't something for the future; it's happening today. We already have complete access to everything He offers. Paul prayed that we would be filled with all the fullness of God.

As this filling happens, it's important to avoid misunderstanding. Like I said earlier, it's not like filling a gas tank with a hose continuously pouring in. Instead, it's more about recognizing, unveiling, and awakening to the fullness that has always been present. We simply weren't aware of it before.

It's all about the presence, about realizing the *parousia*. It's time to stop pushing the Triune God's abiding presence into the future and shift that perspective. We can dwell in His presence now, in the present moment. Sometimes, people live with a hit-and-miss experience of God's presence because they see it as something in the future. I've been in situations where we've prayed earnestly for God's presence to be with us during the service as if He were somewhere else —but that's not truly carrying His presence with us.

LIVING IN THE REALITY OF GOD'S PRESENCE

What if I told you that it's impossible to be outside the presence of God except in your mind?

Ephesians Chapter 2, verse 6 states that He raised us up and made us sit together in the heavenly places in Christ. This isn't just a theory or a concept; it's the truth. You're not outside of His presence; He has placed us with Him in heavenly places. You cannot escape the presence of God, even though it may feel like it. He is everywhere; wherever you go, He's already there. He raised us up and seated us in heavenly places in Christ Jesus.

Colossians 3:3 states, "For you died, and your life is hidden with Christ in God." This is your position; it's not just a potential theory. Paul isn't merely providing interesting teachings or revelations for us to admire; he wants us to *experience* them. Until we're ready to embrace this Spirit-to-spirit feeding and allow these truths to be written on our hearts as a fixed reality, they will remain mere concepts.

As the truth is written on your heart, it begins to manifest. Suddenly, you start experiencing, living, and demonstrating it without even saying a word. There's a saying that we should always preach the gospel and use words when necessary. I believe much of what Jesus did was through His actions, without needing to verbalize it. As the Word becomes flesh in us, we start responding automatically to the prompting of the Spirit.

You don't have to consciously think about it anymore; you just respond. When the Holy Spirit says turn right, you turn right; when He says turn left, you turn left, even if it seems better to go straight ahead. You trust His guidance, knowing that every-thing works together for good for those who love God. You may not understand why things happen, but He holds the mystery of the why.

Jesus followed the Spirit every step of the way. He said, "I only do what I see the Father do; I only say what I hear the Father say." This is living from your spirit. Paul wants us to live in

God's presence so we can do likewise. It's not a decision you make once; it's a growing experience.

All these experiences come from within, in Colossians 3:16 it says: "Let the word of Christ dwell in you richly." This isn't just any word; it's the word He speaks to you personally. Allow it full access; don't restrict it or doubt it. Experience the fullness of God. He's trying to fill you up, so don't talk yourself out of it.

FROM INNER STRENGTH TO OUTWARD EXPRESSION

Back to Ephesians 3:16: "That He would grant you, according to the riches of His glory, to be strengthened with might through His Spirit in the inner man." This highlights the inner work happening within us, which ultimately bears fruit outwardly. Ever wondered how to grow the fruit of the Spirit? It begins within and then manifests outwardly. The life must first be within before it can demonstrate outwardly.

Galatians 5:25 emphasizes the connection between our inner and outer lives: "If we live in the Spirit, we should also walk in the Spirit." The living happens *within us*; that's where the process unfolds. It might not always be quick, but as the internal process works, we begin to walk it out externally.

> **Paul's point here is clear:** We live in the Word by the Spirit, and then we bear fruit by walking in daily communion with the presence of Holy Spirit.

His presence nurtures us internally and then manifests outwardly, revealing us as manifested sons of God. It's about yielding to the internal process, allowing the inner life to shape our outer actions.

We've moved beyond religious attempts to change our outer selves because it's impossible to control the flesh with the flesh. Instead, as the life of God, *zoe life*, flows into us through His love, it permeates every aspect of our being, shaping our thoughts, actions, and every part of us. This internal transformation naturally demonstrates itself outwardly.

> Here's what I'm trying to say, and I hope it's coming across clearly: Your inner man governs your outer man.

Romans 8:11 explains that if the same Spirit that raised Jesus from the dead dwells in you, it will give life to your mortal bodies.

Your flesh actually derives its life from the Spirit. As long as your spirit is infused with *zoe life*, the life of God, you cannot perish. That's how God designed it. Paul's message in Ephesians 3:14-21 is about an internal transformation, not your external behavior. That aspect takes care of itself automatically.

LEARNING TO PRACTICE HIS PRESENCE

> If God's presence is within us, as Paul taught the Ephesians, then how do we cultivate it? —through awareness and practice.

His presence is within us and surrounds us, and we develop it by being aware, accepting, agreeing, and acknowledging it. We become aware that we are one with Him, retaining individuality yet sharing the same essence as the Father, the Son, and the Holy Spirit. As Jesus said, "In that day, you'll know that I'm in the Father and you're in me, and I'm in you." We are one with God.

We need to practice being aware of our union; His presence is omnipresent, and we cannot evade it. It fills all and is in all. So, it's essential to reprogram ourselves, and we achieve this by practicing His presence. Brother Lawrence's book, *The Practice of the Presence of God* offers valuable insights into this. The more we strengthen our inner selves and engage in practicing His presence, the more we become aware of Him at all times. Just as you can drive your car without consciously thinking about it because it becomes automatic, we can live life fully aware of His presence even though we're doing other things.

Living in the Spirit requires walking in the Spirit. The realm of His presence that you're experiencing now is a realm you will never depart from. You may fluctuate in and out of awareness, but you will always remain fully enveloped in the Father's presence. Embrace this truth today, knowing that it's absolute. It's your destiny as a son or daughter, it's the ultimate experience of sonship and daughterhood.

7
THE POWER OF IMPARTATION

The life of a *manifested* son or daughter is to impart to others what we have received from God. What sets our generation apart from others is that we see the necessity of building God's kingdom and passing on to the next generation the revelation of the truth we've received to help them build and carry it forward.

Let's dive into Ephesians Chapter 4 with the idea of sharing what God has given us in mind. In this chapter, Paul shows us exactly how to do this within our community. He talks about unity, growing together in faith, and supporting each other — key parts of living out our faith and passing it on. As we move into Ephesians 4, we'll see how these teachings help us build up the church and keep the cycle of impartation going.

LIVING OUT OUR IDENTITY

Verses 1-3: "I, therefore, the prisoner of the Lord, beseech you to walk worthy of the calling with which you were called, with all lowliness and gentleness, with long suffering, bearing with one another in love, endeavoring to keep the unity of the Spirit in the bond of peace."

Paul's letter to the Ephesians gives us a roadmap for our faith journey. In the first three chapters, he shows us the scenic route, saying, "Look at all these amazing gifts you've got! You were chosen, blessed, and loved beyond measure by God Himself before the world even began."

Then, here, in Chapter 4, Paul gets practical. He says, "You know all these amazing things about yourself so now it's time to live like it." It's as though he's pulling up a chair for a heart-to-heart, chat encouraging us to show the world who we really are in Christ.

He's not just talking about acting morally or doing good things. Paul is getting at something deeper. It's about understanding the great things we've been given and sharing those gifts with others, helping them see their identity and purpose.

Paul reminds us that being a Christian isn't just about knowing we're loved and saved; it's about living out that love and salvation in real, tangible ways daily. It's about how we treat our neighbor, how we handle disagreements, and how we support each other in our walk with Christ.

In the first 16 verses of Ephesians 4, Paul explains that understanding our identity in Jesus is just the beginning. The real work is living out that identity through love and unity so we can positively impact our world.

It's more than just holding onto the great things we've learned; it's about sharing these bits of spirit and truth far and wide, immersing others in what we've been immersed in.

THERE IS ONLY ONE SOURCE

> Paul is leading up to something big: He's about to reveal where all this power and mission come from.

Verses 4-5: "*There is* one body and one Spirit, just as you were called in one hope of your calling; one Lord, one faith, one baptism."

Paul is pointing us back to a singular source of life and faith —
the Triune God. He is the point of origination. Everything we
are and everything we have comes from God.

Verse 6: "There is one God and Father of all, who *is* above all,
through all, and in you all."

Recognizing the Father as the ultimate source and originator is
pivotal. He isn't distant; His presence permeates everything.
Paul dispels any notion of duality within us, affirming that God
alone sustains our life, spirit, and mind. This teaching isn't just
theoretical; it's deeply practical. It reassures us of our place in
God's family and underscores our unity with fellow believers.
Embracing and living out this truth, we reflect the unity and
love of our one God and Father, embodying the oneness of the
body of Christ for the world to see.

Verse 7: "But to each one of us grace was given according to the
measure of Christ's gift."

The depth of our understanding of grace is intertwined with
our perception of Jesus — as our comprehension of Jesus
expands, we grow in grace.

Now, starting with verse 8, Paul moves into the practical aspect of impartation. He's laid out the foundational truths in the first seven verses, and now he's ready to teach us how to share these truths with others.

Verse 8: "Therefore, He says, 'When He ascended on high, He led captivity captive and gave gifts to men.'"

And in verses 9 and 10 Paul refers to Jesus ascending after descending into the lower parts of the earth. There's a principle here — to ascend, you must first descend.

CHRIST'S GIFT: THE FIVE-FOLD MINISTRY

Verse 11 unveils the extraordinary and divine gifts that Jesus granted humanity: apostles, prophets, evangelists, pastors, and teachers. These aren't ordinary gifts; they come directly from Jesus and are distinguished as ascension gifts given upon His ascension. Each of these gifts serves a distinct purpose within the church, much like the unique roles of each finger on a hand.

The apostle, for instance, is versatile and capable of stepping into the other functions of prophets, evangelists, pastors, and teachers. Each gift is a divine instrument, crucial in dispensing and imparting the truth to others.

Everyone possesses at least one or some of these gifts within them. For those who value order and structure, who are organized and systematic, there's a touch of apostolic anointing. Apostles excel in church governance, ensuring everything operates efficiently. Prophets, on the other hand, provide guidance and are not as concerned with organization. That's why apostles and prophets form the church's foundation: prophets point the way, while apostles keep things organized and working smoothly.

Evangelists are the outreach arms, drawing people in with signs, wonders, and miracles. They effortlessly connect with people and witness transformation in their lives. Pastors love and feed these individuals. They excel in forming deep, covenant relationships and drawing people close with their love. Teachers provide instruction. Their gift lies in teaching and exhortation, inspiring and guiding others in their journey.

How are we to use these gifts: Equip the saints so that the saints might do the work of the ministry, for the edifying and building up of the body of Christ until we all come to the unity of the faith and to the knowledge of the Son of God, to become perfect men to the measure of the stature of the fullness of Christ.

> Have we arrived at unity in faith? Are we at the point where we all possess a mature understanding of the Son of God, embodying the full stature of Christ's perfection?

The straightforward answer is no. We haven't gotten there yet. That's why these five gifts — apostles, prophets, evangelists, pastors, and teachers — remain essential for us today.

However, there are a few things we need to unpack and clarify about these five roles.

These gifts are not meant to elevate some believers into superstar status above others. The idea that these gifts place some above others as if they were elite members of the kingdom and the rest of us merely their servants is a misunderstanding that has hurt the body of Christ. In truth, these roles are designed to serve the entire community of believers. Each of us carries a part of these gifts, signifying that we all have significant roles to fulfill within the body of Christ.

The key is to share what we've been given to others. This passage highlights the importance of imparting — sharing kingdom truths, principles, and power from one individual to another.

As outlined in verses 15 and 16, the goal is to speak the truth in love and grow up into Christ, who is the Head. The entire body is joined and knit together by what every joint supplies. In other words, when each body part plays its role, it creates growth, building itself up in love.

Living out this message of love, inclusion, mercy, and reconciliation begins with a deep personal understanding and belief in these principles. Only once we fully grasp and embody these truths can we effectively share them with others. Our goal is to supply and build up the body of Christ through the transference or impartation of kingdom truth and principles.

EMBRACING THE PURE FLOW OF IMPARTATION

Grasping the full measure of grace given to us and the greatness of Jesus in our lives is the essential starting point for impartation. Think about it: the God Jesus revealed in His incarnation is beyond any religion, any doctrine, and yes, even beyond the pages of a book. Until you see the Father as being in all, being the Father of everybody, the flow of impartation will be limited. Despite this, a pure flow of impartation persists even in the clutter.

We've obstructed the channel of pure impartation with religion, personal motives, and the pursuit of building ministries rather than serving people. By elevating preachers to superstar status, we've created a division between them and the congregation, categorizing one group as 'haves' and the other as 'have-nots.' Portraying ministry as an arena solely for the elite distorts its true essence. The journey of sonship entails constant transformation, with every change facilitated through impartation.

UNDERSTANDING THE DYNAMICS OF IMPARTATION

> Impartation can occur in two ways: Directly from the Spirit of Truth through Spirit-to-spirit revelation or through other individuals.

Verse 16, which speaks of joints supplying and each joint building up the whole body, refers to impartation from one person to another. While verse 7 discusses receiving an accurate measure of the gift of Christ, impartation often comes through the Spirit of Truth when no one is available to impart the necessary grace. Both are essential; don't focus solely on one or the other. Some people reject human teaching, believing they don't need it, while others rely solely on human teaching and overlook the guidance of the Spirit. For growth, you require both dimensions of impartation.

What we're witnessing in this present movement is a journey into a deeper spiritual realm, a transition towards awakened awareness, and a life that transcends ordinary boundaries. As you receive from this deeper spiritual dimension, you can impart it to others. Through your actions and words, the invisible kingdom within you becomes visible.

The kingdom within is built when you're open to receiving impartation. Resistance to receiving keeps the kingdom within underdeveloped, limiting your ability to extend it to others.

In Matthew 13:11-12, Jesus makes an intriguing statement: "Because it has been given to you to know the mysteries of the kingdom of heaven...For whoever has, to him more will be given, and he will have abundance."

In the kingdom, you're either progressing or regressing; stagnation feels like moving backward while others advance. If that's how you're feeling, I challenge you to pursue and embrace what the Spirit of Truth reveals In doing that you'll receive even more.

Remember, communication and impartation are intertwined. With every communication, whether through words or actions, you impart your thoughts, values, and attitudes. Sharing negativity transmits fear or panic. This is why it's important to be selective about who has access to your inner life and influences you. Communication and impartation are closely linked. Whenever someone communicates with you, they impart something, so it's vital to be discerning about what you accept.

From this point forward, everything revolves around your ability to both receive and give impartation. The communication flows from the Spirit to you, from others to you, or from you to other people. It's a spirit-to-spirit exchange discerned by the spirit within you. You must learn to discern it in this manner.

Every good thing from the Father comes through impartation, not through effort or striving. It flows from the Spirit to your spirit and through people, and then when you impart what you've received, you give back to others. We are living in an extraordinary time of revelation. The flow of revelation is rapid and powerful, like an unstoppable river. Even in your sleep, the Spirit of God is at work in your life.

The influx of revelation may feel overwhelming at times, like a tsunami wave. But I encourage you to embrace it like a master surfer — ride the wave, allowing it to carry you forward with grace and wisdom.

8

TRANSCENDING ORDINARY EXISTENCE

I f the beliefs we hold and the revelations we see are not manifested in our lives, what purpose do they serve? Like you, I want to see my beliefs come to fruition, living as a *manifested* son of God and encouraging others to do the same.

In this chapter, I'll take Paul's words and show how they can fit into our lives today. Just as Paul tailored his teaching for his audience, I want to do the same for our modern way of living.

In Ephesians Chapter 4, verses 7-32, Paul contrasts their past behaviors and the new life that flows naturally from living in the Spirit.

UNCOVERING A GENTILE MENTALITY

Ephesians 4:17: "This I say, therefore, and testify in the Lord, that you should no longer walk as the rest of the Gentiles walk, in the futility of their mind."

The word 'futility' is *mataiotés* in the original Greek text and refers to something unproductive or ineffective. Paul is talking about what I like to refer to as the 'Gentile mentality,' and it produces a lifestyle marked by inefficiency and unproductivity.

> This mindset isn't exclusive to non-believers; even believers can fall into it. Despite knowing truth, we might find ourselves stuck in old mental habits, leading to frustration because of the unfruitful outcomes these habits yield.

It's surprising how many theories exist about everything, including God. Some equate Him with mythological, pagan figures like Zeus, while others portray Him as lacking power or victory, leaving the job half done, requiring us to finish it.

Luke 19:10 declares Jesus' mission to seek and save the lost. Yet, in our religious interpretations, we've reshaped this image into one where Jesus searches for the lost but appears lacks the power to fully save them without our help. This flawed interpretation has resulted in fragmented theology, evidenced by the existence of over 40,000 denominations. Each claims to follow Christ and uphold the Bible as their foundational authority. Yet, this vast array of beliefs, stemming from our collective misunderstanding, has only served to further divide us. This is the outcome of a futile mind — a Gentile mentality — that has led us to a state of unproductivity and ineffectiveness.

In verse 18, Paul paints a vivid picture for the Ephesians, revealing the grim reality of succumbing to a futile mindset.

Verse 18: "Having their understanding darkened, being alienated from the life of God, because of the ignorance that is in them, because of the blindness of their heart."

It's a life shrouded in shadows, where the light of understanding struggles to break through. It's a feeling of self-imposed isolation from the vibrant life we are designed to enjoy with the Triune God, trapped in the clutches of ignorance and a heart veiled in darkness.

I love the Passion Translation of verse 18: "Their corrupted logic has been clouded because their hearts are so far from God —their blinded understanding and deep-seated moral darkness keeps them from the true knowledge of God."

In His infinite wisdom, God has been steadily removing the darkness we walk in, illuminating a fuller understanding of who He is. Today, knowledge and revelation are not just trickling in but pouring into God's people. This is not just remarkable, it's a beacon of light that should fill us with excitement and empowerment!

In verses 17 and 18, Paul points out a disconnect between the lifestyle some live and the teachings he shared in the first three chapters. He reinforces this point in verse 20, declaring, 'You have not so learned Christ.'

Verses 20-24: "But you have not so learned Christ, if indeed you have heard Him and have been taught by Him, as the truth is in Jesus: that you put off, concerning your former conduct, the old man which grows corrupt according to the deceitful lusts, and be renewed in the spirit of your mind, and that you put on the new man which was created according to God, in true righteousness and holiness."

He urges believers to align their lives with the truth they have learned in Christ. He reminds them of their new identity and calls for a transformative renewal of their minds. Rather than persisting in old behaviors, they are encouraged to embrace their new selves, created in the image of God — righteous and holy.

TRANSFORMING THE MIND: FROM OLD TO NEW

Paul's message is unmistakable: Leave the old self behind and step into the new.

This concept is not just limited to his Ephesian teachings but is echoed in the book of Colossians as well. Specifically, in Colossians 1:13, he presents a similar idea, though phrased slightly different. There, he tells us we've been rescued from darkness and moved into the light of God's kingdom, symbolizing the shedding of the 'old man' and embracing the 'new man.' This transition is about recognizing our deliverance from a life of corruption and stepping into a life marked by righteousness and holiness.

Before diving any deeper, in verses 25 and 26, Paul emphasizes the detrimental impact of corrupt thinking and the negative lifestyle it produces.

> This point is so crucial I might repeat it throughout this teaching: *Your thought patterns directly influence your way of life.*

Simply put, incorrect thinking leads to incorrect living.

Verses 25-26: "Therefore, putting away lying, 'Let each one of you speak truth with his neighbor,' for we are members of one another. Be angry and sin not. Do not let the sun go down on your wrath."

Then, moving on to verse 29, Paul provides a concrete example of how the corrupt mindset — the 'old man' — actually appears in our actions and behaviors.

Verse 29-31: "Let no corrupt word proceed out of your mouth, but what is good for necessary edification, that it may impart grace to the hearers. And do not grieve the Holy Spirit of God, by whom you were sealed for the day of redemption. Let all bitterness, wrath, anger, clamor, and evil speaking be put away from you, with all malice."

These verses vividly depict the manifestations of the 'old man' in our lives, echoing the mindset described in verses 17 and 18 — a Gentile mentality characterized by spiritual blindness, toxic thoughts, feelings of separation from God, and ignorance or spiritual blindness. This portrayal illustrates how such a mindset translates into our daily lives, revealing that wrong thinking leads to wrong behaviors. However, the focus here isn't solely on changing our behaviors; it's on the transformation or renewal of our minds.

Going back to verse 27, Paul introduces a concept that may initially seem unexpected but is not as out of place as one might think. Paul highlights a crucial point in verse 27. Here, he advises, "Neither give place to the devil," suggesting a direct link between the devil and the patterns of thought and behavior he's been warning against. Paul links the devil directly to the issues of spiritual blindness, futile thinking, and distorted thought patterns. He emphasizes that the devil's influence is not so much in actions but in the corrupt thought processes.

Now, I want to challenge you to do something in scripture. While it may not apply universally, in many instances, replacing 'the devil' or 'satan' with 'carnal mind' can open up new insights.

Applying this to verse 27 shows how well it fits with Paul's message. Consider reading it as 'neither give place to the carnal mind.' Carnal thinking is part of the futile mindset Paul describes in verse 17. It's also part of the lifestyle depicted in verses 25, 26, and 29 to 31.

As mentioned, it's not always possible to replace 'devil' or 'satan' with 'carnal mind' in every scriptural instance. However, in many cases, this substitution is fitting. The word 'devil' is derived from the Greek word *diabolos*, meaning a slanderous accuser. This term can also imply a deceiver or adversary. Frequently, our own mind becomes our most significant accuser, inundating us with feelings of condemnation and doubt above all else.

By reinterpreting 'neither give place to the devil' as 'neither give place to carnal thinking,' we uncover a deeper truth. Carnal thinking embodies slanderous accusation, deception, and adversity — it is the manifestation of a mind driven by fleshly desires. In stark contrast, renewing our minds liberates us from deceit and self-accusation, effectively countering the adversary within.

RENEWING THE SPIRIT OF THE MIND: PUTTING ON THE NEW MAN

Paul doesn't just identify the problem; he offers a solution as well. While he does caution us against letting these negative influences take root by not giving space to 'the carnal mind' or the 'devil,' he also assures us in verse 23 that there is an anti-dote, a way to prevent giving any ground to our internal adversary.

Verse 23: "Be renewed in the spirit of your mind."

Paul didn't simply instruct us to renew our minds or to adopt a new mindset. He said, "Be renewed in the spirit of your mind." This distinction is of utmost importance. Paul isn't merely advocating for a superficial change of thoughts; he is calling for a deep renewal of our inner reasoning and understanding — the mind, or *nous*, as it is called in Greek. He urges us to undergo a transformation at the very core of our being, not just in our mind, but in the *spirit* of our mind. Be renewed in the spirit of what causes you to reason and understand things.

Paul isn't talking here about simply reading a book and changing your mind or upgrading your thinking on some level. He's not merely suggesting thinking differently or adding more information, theories, or concepts. It's not an academic or intellectual exercise; that's not what Paul is emphasizing. The 'spirit of your mind' is the driving force, the source of empowered thinking. Paul is urging us to disconnect from what has been empowering our thinking and to connect to another source. Just acquiring more head knowledge or going through the motions won't accomplish this transformation.

> The Spirit of God within us erases our old way of thinking and reprogram us so that a new spirit governs our life. What does that look like? We put on the new man!

Verse 24: "And that you put on the new man which was created according to God, in true righteousness and holiness."

Paul said in verse 24 that we are to *put on* the new man. The new man, which was created according to God in true righteousness and holiness, is our source of power and strength. The key lies in immersing yourself entirely in our new God-shaped identity, embracing the understanding and life we have awakened to. This entails allowing the image and likeness of God within you to become the predominant influence on your reasoning and understanding.

Instead of being driven by the old ways of thinking, characteristic of the Gentile mentality, we are to shift our focus to the righteousness and true holiness inherent in our new identity. Therefore, allowing this divine image to govern and empower your thinking, reasoning, and understanding.

Throughout our lives, we've been programmed to think a certain way because we've been hypnotized by the carnal mind. We've been mesmerized into believing that we're just ordinary men incapable of ever being more than that. As a result, we've developed amnesia regarding the true source of our thinking and what should be the life source of our minds.

Let's make this practical. In Ephesians 4:17-30, Paul teaches that when your mind is empowered by the right source, you'll live in alignment with righteousness and experience a full, fulfilled, and God-centered life. As you are renewed in the spirit of your mind — not your intellect — but the spirit of your mind, you move out of a Gentile mentality and begin to exercise the mind of Christ.

It's important to believe that you possess the mind of Christ, as affirmed in 1 Corinthians 2:16, "We have the mind of Christ." Learning to trust, rely on, and rest in it is essential, knowing that your thoughts reflect the mind of Christ within you. If the thoughts you entertain do not align with the mind of Christ, the Spirit within you will prompt you, leading you away from the old way of thinking.

In Matthew Chapter 7, Jesus emphasizes the importance concerning what influences our thinking and how our minds should operate.

BUILDING ON THE ROCK: EMBODYING JESUS' TEACHINGS

Matthew 7:24: "Therefore whoever hears these sayings of Mine, and does them, I will liken him to a wise man who built his house on the rock."

Jesus underscores the importance of not just hearing His words but also actively applying them. This act of listening and then embodying His teachings is what it means to put on the new man. When you hear what God communicates to you and actively apply it to your life, that message becomes a part of who you are. When you put the sayings of Jesus into practice in your life, your foundation is built on the Rock; it's unshakable. Even when the rains descend, the floods arise, and the winds blow and beat against your house, it will not fall, for it is founded on the Rock.

Jesus continues and compares another to a foolish builder whose house is built on the sand. When storms hit, that house couldn't stand and tragically collapsed. This reflects how many of us might have lived before — acknowledging Jesus' teachings without fully understanding or applying them. It's like saying, "I've heard His words, but didn't know how to live by them. I didn't make them a reality in my life." This lack of application and manifestation leads to a weak and vulnerable foundation, unable to withstand life's challenges.

Jesus uses the analogy of two houses to represent two distinct lives: one embraces the new self, marked by righteousness and holiness, while the other clings to the old way of thinking, the Gentile mentality.

Despite facing identical challenges — rain, wind, and storms — each life reacts differently. The life built on the teachings of Jesus, on the solid foundation of the new self, not only withstands these trials but also emerges stronger, ready to face future storms confidently. This analogy beautifully illustrates the contrast between a life that folds under pressure and one that stands firm, knowing it can withstand the storm. Jesus' teaching here resonates deeply with Paul's message about putting off the old man and putting on the new.

The choice to either build on the rock or the sand is yours. The wise man embodies kingdom principles, living in alignment with who they are in Christ. In contrast, the foolish man represents a Gentile mentality. This foolish man might possess some knowledge and insight, but he fails to apply it, make it manifest in his life, and truly live by it.

TRANSFORMATIVE ONENESS

In John 10:30, when Jesus says, "I and my Father are one," he shares a fundamental transforamtive teaching that is the cornerstone for understanding this principle characterized by renewing the spirit of your mind. Embracing this truth empowers you and reshapes your thought processes. When this understanding permeates your being, you transcend the limitations of the old man.

This declaration, 'I and my Father are one,' is not just empowering; it's revolutionary. It challenges the status quo, particularly the religious establishment, which thrives on control. It's a direct threat to institutional power, signaling a shift towards spiritual autonomy and enlightenment. It infuriated the religious leaders of Jesus' day. Verse 31 says, "the Jews took up stones again to stone Him." This act illustrates the threat Jesus' teachings posed to traditional religious authority.

In today's context, the "stones" may not be literal but verbal criticisms or attacks. Embracing and living out the truth of oneness with the Father — moving beyond the idea of God being distant to a face-to-face union — provokes strong reactions from those entrenched in religious norms. This concept challenges conventional views, leading to questions like, "Who do you think you are?" from those unable to accept such a complete union with the Father.

Following the intense reaction in verse 31, Jesus responds in verse 32 by questioning the religious leaders: "I have shown you many good works from the Father. For which of these do you stone me?" This response exemplifies the strength of an empowered mind. Despite facing hostility and the threat of violence, Jesus does not waver. This unwavering stance, even as metaphorical storms rage around him, showcases the solid foundation on which He stands — a deep understanding of His absolute oneness with the Father.

In verse 33, the religious leaders explicitly state their reason for wanting to stone Jesus: not for any good deed but for blasphemy. This was scandalous!! Jesus' assertion challenged conventional religious boundaries because when one professes, "The Father and I are one," it transcends mere human identity, venturing into the realm of divine identity. This is the very revelation Jesus aimed to bring us into — a realization of our humanity as the new creation that far exceeds the limited view often portrayed by a Gentile mentality.

Paul reflects on this in Philippians 2, indicating that Jesus did not consider it blasphemous or wrong to see Himself as equal with God. Jesus fully embraced His identity, embodying the fullness of the Godhead bodily. Unlike us, Jesus didn't have an "old man" to discard; He lived entirely from a "new man" perspective, fully empowered and enlightened by His complete union with the Father.

To shift their perspective, Jesus attempts to renew the spirit of their minds. In verse 34, He challenges their understanding with, "Is it not written in your law, 'I have said you are gods?'" While some might seek to reinterpret this statement to fit within narrow religious confines, the essence of His message is clear. Though the term has a lowercase 'g,' its significance is remarkable. Jesus isn't suggesting we are the vast ocean but rather, a cup drawn from it. This metaphor implies that even a small portion shares the same DNA, characteristics, and potential as the whole.

Jesus isn't claiming we are the Creator but rather, that we are partakers of the divine nature. We have the characteristics of God. Jesus elaborates in verse 35, saying, "If He called them gods, to whom the word of God came and the Scripture cannot be broken."

> This is what Paul was trying to drive home in Ephesians 4:17-32 when he said, "Put on the new man!" In other words, realize and live from who you are in Christ.

Putting on the new man before challenges arise sets a solid foundation, so when life's inevitable storms hit, you remain unshaken and firmly planted in the revelation that you and the Father are one.

The reality is that your life reflects what's been cultivated in your mind; the experiences and situations you encounter today are a result of the perspectives and beliefs you've adopted from a Gentile mentality and the world around you.

GUARDING THE HEART: CULTIVATING SEEDS OF REALITY

Proverbs 4:23 says, "Guard your heart above all else, for it is the source of life" (CSB). What your mind feeds into your heart will manifest in your life. This principle can be expressed in various forms: whatever your soul feeds into your spirit will come to fruition. Likewise, what your conscious mind imparts to your subconscious will also materialize.

Your heart functions like a garden, capable of cultivating any seed sown within it. Therefore, when your mind plants seeds of fear, they will grow. Similarly, seeds of doubt and insecurity sown will also take root and flourish. It's important to remember that the heart does not have a mind of its own.

This underscores the freedom that comes with renewing the spirit of our mind. It serves as the driving force, sowing the seeds of our reality. The key is to cultivate a constant awareness of God, understanding our oneness with Him which becomes the driving force of the spirit of our mind. Embracing this belief revolutionizes our lives. We realize we no longer need to spend countless hours seeking God's presence or pleading for Him to be with us as if His presence were something external to be obtained.

He is always with us, a constant presence in our lives, not because we have called Him into our moments but because we are one with Him. Realizing that we are perpetually in union with God eliminates the need for pleading or bargaining. This revelation transforms our spiritual life, assuring us we no longer need to beg for what is already ours in Christ.

Jesus never approached prayer as a means to acquire something. He didn't calm the storm or multiply loaves and fishes by claiming it through faith alone. Instead, He exercised dominion, fully aware of His intrinsic union with Father. This was the foundation of all He did, including prayer. This realization of oneness, of complete union, is what empowered Him.

> This should also be your declaration: "To see me is to see the Father!"

It's time for a shift in perspective, embracing our union with Father, Son, and Holy Spirit as the basis for how we live and interact with the world around us.

It's not merely that God is resides within me, within you, or scattered throughout humanity. Instead, think of it like this: God is revealing Himself to the world *through* each of us. When you see me, you're catching a glimpse of God, just as seeing you reveals Him. We are all unique manifestations of God's presence in the world.

The time has passed for depending on a far-off God, whose responses and presence might feel uncertain. He never wished for us to live in such separation. We're invited to actively participate in our relationship with Him, shaping our reality by the intentions and beliefs we cultivate within our hearts, spirits, or subconscious minds. The seeds we plant and nurture within us will determine what grows and becomes manifest in our lives.

A RENEWED MIND: EMBRACING THE MIND OF CHRIST

A renewed spirit of the mind believes that we possess the mind of Christ. When the desires of your mind drop into your heart, they become the desires of your heart. Your spirit goes into super-production mode to manifest what you have fed into your spirit.

So, what are you desiring in life? A life filled with kingdom abundance? If that's not your current reality, it's time to start planting the seeds of your deepest desires into your heart or spirit. It's God who works in you both to will and to do of His good pleasure. He put those desires into your heart.

When the Spirit infuses and energizes my thinking, my mind is renewed. I realize that I can do nothing of myself, yet I also acknowledge that I can do all things through Christ.

Do you grasp the significance of this? Jesus said, "I, of my own self, can do nothing, but what I see the Father do, I do." He also acknowledged that He couldn't say anything of His own accord, but only what He heard the Father say.

Don, that's all good for Jesus, but what about me? Jesus answers this in John 14:20, pulling us into this divine equation. He said, 'In that day' — 2,000 years ago—'you will realize that I am in my Father, and you are in me, and I am in you.' So, He not only shares His intimate union with the Father but extends it to us, including us in this inseparable, face-to-face relationship He has with the Father.

This is a deep, perspective-shifting, life-altering truth! Meditate on it. Chew on it during quiet moments or while driving instead of filling that time with music or news. Reflect on Jesus' words: "You in Me, and I in you." Let this realization sink in deeply, transforming your understanding until it becomes as integral to your being as any foundational belief. This is the essence of building your life on a steadfast, unshakeable foundation, as Jesus taught.

In John 17:22-24, Jesus prays a prayer that reflects His deep connection with the Father and His aspiration for His followers to share in that same unity, glory, and love. He prays for us to be enveloped in the same divine joy and love that has existed between Him and the Father from before the creation of the world. This prayer is not just a hopeful desire but a bold request for divine oneness: 'I in them, and You in Me, that they may be made perfect in one.' Through this, Jesus envisions a spiritual unity that transcends individual existence apart from Him, drawing all believers into His perfect wholeness.

Moreover, Jesus doesn't seek our removal from the world's challenges; instead, He requests divine protection for us against evil (John 17:15). He assures us that we are sent into the world as He was — fully equipped and completely empowered to overcome any obstacle. This readiness and empowerment are the foundation on which we should build our lives.

The days of mechanically reciting Bible verses to strengthen faith are behind us. We are now beckoned to a deeper understanding and connection with God's Spirit — a Spirit-to-spirit connection — which illuminates our minds and saturates our lives with the essence of divine truth. This transformative process transcends mere intellectual agreement to a profound internalization, where these truths materialize in our actions and being.

> Jesus' prayer calls us to recognize our divine nature, reminding us of the scriptural assertion, "Aren't you gods?" This isn't just a rhetorical question — it's a direct acknowledgment of our inherent divinity and potential.

Divinity is our identity in Christ! When we embrace this as our reality, we move beyond seeing ourselves as merely ordinary — created in the image and likeness of God means we are anything but ordinary.

Acknowledging our unity with the Triune God shapes how we live from this moment forward. This is the era of embodying Christ, living as spiritual beings in human form, and fully realizing our divine identity. Embrace this shift and live out your divine nature to its fullest.

9
MANIFESTING DIVINE TRUTHS

In Chapter five of Ephesians, Paul continues his focus on the tangible expression of the truths from his first three chapters into our daily lives. Acting as a wise mentor, he urges us not to merely embrace these truths in theory but to wear them like a cloak, integrating them fully into the fabric of our lives.

He's not advocating for a superficial checklist of righteousness; instead, he invites us into a deeper, more authentic way of living out the divine blueprint of our identity that he meticulously laid out in the preceding chapters. Chapters four, five, and six of Ephesians offer a vivid portrait of how our lives can unfold in grace and truth when we deeply absorb the essence of Paul's words from the initial chapters.

It isn't merely about adopting a new set of behaviors but about undergoing a deep internal transformation. What Paul has imparted in the first three chapters becomes the heartbeat of our existence. Our lives naturally and effortlessly reflect these truths as we internalize his teachings on identity, sonship, and divine love. It's a journey from understanding to becoming, where the wisdom of these earlier chapters doesn't just stay lodged in our minds but flourishes through our actions and interactions, becoming as integral to us as our own breath.

Sometimes, it's easy to drift slightly off course in our understanding of grace, mistakenly equating it with inaction. However, if my own journey — filled with teaching, studying, traveling, and ministering more than ever before — is anything to go by, it's clear that grace does not exempt us from action. Instead, it redefines the purpose behind our actions

.

Grace doesn't mean we stop acting; rather, it teaches us that our actions aren't about earning favor or proving our worth. We act not to gain grace but from a place of grace already bestowed upon us. This understanding doesn't diminish our actions; it transforms them. It redirects our motivations from striving to earn love to responding to the love we've already received, guiding us in how we live, love, and serve.

A CALL TO WALK IN LOVE

Let's dive into Chapter five.

Paul masterfully weaves together a series of verses that, while distinct, share a common thread of thought. He shows us how to live out this message effectively and powerfully. In the first verse of this chapter, Paul encourages us to let these teachings truly shape our actions and interactions, turning our everyday experiences into a dynamic demonstration of who we are in Christ.

Ephesians 5:1: "Therefore, be imitators of God as dear children."

While this seems simple, the word 'imitate' can suggest just copying actions, not capturing the full spirit of what it means. A more fitting word would be 'reflect' or 'mirror.' To reflect or mirror God means our actions come from a deep understanding of our oneness with God and that we are embodiments of His love and grace. This isn't just about doing what God does — it's about reflecting the perfect image of who He is.

In verse two, he explains how we can effectively reflect and mirror God.

Verse 2: "And walk in love, as Christ also has loved us and given Himself for us, an offering and a sacrifice to God for a sweet-smelling aroma."

Love must become preeminent in our lives for us to start mirroring God accurately. The message of love, long taught in our churches — urging us to love each other and God with all of our hearts —is experiencing a revival. It's as though love is penetrating deeper into our beings than ever before, manifesting with renewed strength and depth. To mirror the Father, we must actively live out this message of love. It must become the cornerstone of our existence. Paul teaches us that when we love like Christ we extend grace and forgiveness to those who have wronged us or caused us pain.

It's not uncommon to encounter situations that leave us questioning the actions and motives of others, leading to hurt and the temptation to shut others out. Yet, Paul's message is clear: erecting barriers is not how we reflect God's love. Instead, we're called to a love that transcends personal grievances and mirrors the selfless love Christ displayed, even to the point of the cross. This level of love — capable of embracing even those who mistreat or misunderstand us — is the true reflection of the Father's heart. But the message of love isn't merely about loving difficult people; it's about allowing love to reshape us, maturing us as sons, empowering us to live and love like Christ.

REFLECTING GOD'S NATURE

In verses 3 to 7, Paul shifts focus, presenting a contrast by illustrating behaviors that do not reflect God's nature. In these verses, Paul effectively says, "Having outlined the path to walking in love, let me now guide you away from actions and attitudes that diverge from this calling." This section acts as a mirror of its own, reflecting what to avoid as we purpose to live out the love we have received and are called to share.

Verse 3-7: "But fornication and all uncleanness or covetousness, let it not even be named among you, as is fitting for saints; neither filthiness, nor foolish talking, nor coarse jesting, which are not fitting, but rather giving of thanks. For this you know, that no fornicator, unclean person, nor covetous man, who is an idolater, has any inheritance in the kingdom of Christ and God. Let no one deceive you with empty words, for because of these things the wrath of God comes upon the sons of disobedience. Therefore do not be partakers with them."

These verses highlight behaviors that not only misrepresent the kingdom but also prevent us from experiencing its benefits here and now. This discussion is not about who enters heaven or faces eternal punishment; it's not concerned with eternal destiny at all. Instead, Paul emphasizes how our actions can disrupt our enjoyment of the kingdom's blessings in our current lives. He underscores that the kingdom is not merely a future promise but a present reality. Our actions can either enhance or hinder our experience of its richness in the here and now.

Paul notes that those engaging in certain actions face God's wrath. However, it's crucial to understand that *God is love*, and everything He does is rooted in love. Wrath, in this context, is not anger, hostility, or hate, but an incredibly intense form of emotional response. Essentially, Paul reveals that the most powerful emotion God can demonstrate is love. Therefore, when individuals engage in behaviors that don't align with His kingdom, God's response is not punitive anger but rather an intensified expression of love.

Remember, it is His goodness that leads us to repentance. When God intensifies His love, we encounter an even greater experience of His love and forgiveness. God is never seeking to push people away. In verses three to seven, Paul is pointing out behaviors that do not mirror or reflect His life in us and ultimately prevent us from fully experiencing the abundant life He desires for us here on earth. God's approach is to envelop us in an even stronger love than we've ever known, shining His goodness so brightly that it leads to an "aha" moment, prompting a heartfelt change.

When the truths of Ephesians Chapters 1-3 are fully integrated into your life, engaging in the behaviors mentioned in verses 3-7 becomes as unthinkable for you as it would for Jesus. These behaviors are misaligned with who you are; they represent a mistaken identity.

> This is a key point: Those who still engage in such actions lack a deep understanding of who they are in Christ.

They have yet to grasp that they have been in Christ since the foundation of the world. Engaging in such behaviors like those Paul describes in these verses are fundamentally out of sync with our true identity in Christ. This isn't about adhering to a set of rules but about the natural expression of our lives as sons.

Beautifully encapsulated in Titus 2:11-12 is the revelation that grace, which has appeared to all men bringing salvation, instructs us to live righteous, holy, and blameless lives in this world. For it is grace that actively teaches and transforms us. It pulls us away from the missteps of verses 3-7, not by ignoring or condoning them but by empowering us to live in a manner that truly reflects and manifests the Father's presence in the world. Grace is not a passive acceptance but a dynamic force that equips us to mirror the Triune God in our everyday lives.

When you mirror the Father by walking in love, your thoughts, actions, and character begin to truly reflect Him. The chains and bonds that have obscured your true identity and prevented the full expression of who you are start to fall away. And they do so naturally, effortlessly, without toil or striving.

PRACTICAL GUIDANCE FOR LIVING WISELY AND SPIRITUALLY

Now, within verses 15 to 21, Paul shifts to offering some really practical advice.

Verses 15-18: "See then that you walk circumspectly, not as fools but as wise, redeeming the time, because the days are evil. Therefore do not be unwise, but understand what the will of the Lord *is*. And do not be drunk with wine, in which is dissipation; but be filled with the Spirit."

The word 'circumspectly' might not be frequently used today, but it simply means to walk carefully.

And the word 'dissipation' refers to the wasteful expenditure of energy and time. By advising against drunkenness, Paul isn't prohibiting wine but warning against overindulgence and its potential to deplete our resources—time, energy, and money. He emphasizes the importance of wisdom, urging us to recognize the moral complexities and challenges of the world. We must avoid allowing these negative influences to dominate our lives as they can detract us from our wisdom and purpose.

Paul concludes verse 18 with a vital directive: "But be filled with the Spirit." This shifts the focus from simply avoiding unwise actions to actively seeking a life led and enriched by the Spirit. It serves as a bridge from merely dodging evil influences to embracing a lifestyle guided and invigorated by the Spirit, demonstrating how we should live empowered by the Spirit and reflect our true identity and redemption.

Verses 19-20: "Speaking to one another in psalms and hymns and spiritual songs. Giving thanks always for all things to God the Father in the name of our Lord Jesus Christ."

This means we should interact in ways that build each other up. In simpler terms, always speak positively to one another. Paul also teaches us to be thankful in all circumstances — adopting gratitude as a mindset, an attitude, and a way of life.

Even in difficult times, he urges us to praise God, thank Him, and let our lives reflect God's character.

Verse 21: "Submitting to one another in the fear of the Lord."

Remember that all of this is a manifestation of the Spirit, as the latter part of verse 18 reminds us. This transformation is not due to our own efforts or initiative. As verse 18 concludes with 'Be filled with the Spirit,' it caps off the teachings of Chapters 1-3. This is a constant reminder that we are not the architects of our spiritual journey. When the teachings from these Chapters are deeply embedded in us, the life described in verses 18b through 21 is not a struggle but an effortless outflow of the Spirit's working within us.

PAUL'S MARRIAGE METAPHOR: CHRIST AND THE CHURCH

Paul continues in verse 22 by showing us how our union with Christ and the manifested life we've been discussing unfolds. Honestly, I hesitated to include this part, aware of how it has been misused to oppress women, twisting its message into a mandate for unquestioning submission within marriage.

This misinterpretation suggests women are incapable of thinking for themselves and must be strictly guided by their husbands, a view that distorts the passage's true meaning.

Much like a parable that extracts spiritual truths from everyday contexts, Paul uses a familiar analogy to convey a deeper, spiritual principle. In this light, we will explore this section as Paul likely intended—as a symbolic illustration, not as a tool for subjugation.

Paul underscores the core message of these 10 verses, urging us to grasp the deeper meaning behind his words.

Verse 32: "I'm speaking to you a great mystery."

Through metaphor, Paul reveals a spiritually deep and mysterious truth. He uses the well-known relationship between a husband and wife not to focus on marriage but to shed light on the deeper union between Christ and the Church.

Sometimes, to clarify a point in a parable, as Paul does here in a mystical way, details might be exaggerated to make them larger than life. This ensures the core message is prominent. The essential message, as Paul highlights in verse 32, focuses on the relationship between Christ and the Church. It's important to read this through the lens of that relationship. While the marriage analogy may seem overstated, this exaggeration is intentional, crafted to underscore the deep, mystical, spiritual connection between Christ and the Church.

Let's dive into verse 22 with this perspective.

SACRED SURRENDER: MUTUAL YIELDING

Verse 22: "Wives, submit yourselves to your own husbands, as to the Lord."

In discussing the relationship between Christ and the Church, Paul illustrates a mutual yielding similar to what is found in marriage. This mutual yielding — a reciprocal giving and receiving — cultivates a deep union. It's essential to recognize that the love exchange between Christ and the Church, and also ideally in marriage, is not about keeping score or dividing efforts 50/50. Instead, it involves complete participation: 100/100. Christ extends His all — 100 percent love — to the Church, and in response, the Church is to respond with its entire being — 100 percent.

Initiated by Christ's unconditional love, this relationship sets a foundation for how we love; we love because He first loved us.

Our love for Him is a response to His action, not a condition of His affection. He does not wait for us to 'submit' before He loves; He loves freely and fully, inviting us to reciprocate the same way. This shifts the relationship from transactional to transformational, where love is not earned but freely given and reciprocated. Paul emphasizes that the Lord's love for us is whole and complete, and our response should mirror that totality.

Verse 23: "For the husband is head of the wife, as also Christ is head of the church; and He is the Savior of the body."

Just as Christ entirely dedicates His life to the Church — His body — without expecting anything in return, Paul parallels the marriage relationship, suggesting that husbands should embody the same selfless devotion towards their wives. The model of unconditional giving, as exemplified by Christ, serves as a guiding principle that empowers us to take action. In verse 23, Paul underscores the importance of living out these principles in our relationships, encouraging us to reflect Christ's selfless love in our interactions with one another.

Verse 24: "Therefore, just as the church is subject to Christ, so let the wives be to their own husbands in everything."

The interpretation of verse 24 has often been misconstrued, leading to the erroneous notion that wives are expected to blindly submit to their husbands without regard for their own will or intellect. However, Paul's true intention diverges from such a narrow understanding. He draws a parallel between the relationship of the Church and Christ, highlighting the importance of willingly aligning ourselves with the mind of Christ in all aspects of life. This alignment does not entail forfeiting our individuality; rather, it involves embracing the transformative power of Christ's mind, which ultimately leads to a more fulfilling and Christ-centered existence.

Paul's message in verse 24 is essentially about the Church experiencing the fullness of what Jesus gave us — our complete inheritance. As we yield to Him, we enjoy what He has given us.

CHRISTLIKE LOVE: SELFLESS

Verse 25: "Husbands, love your wives, just as Christ also loved the church and gave Himself for her."

This love that Paul talks about is one that tenderly cares for and shields the Church. It's a love so deep that Christ won't allow harm to come to us, ensuring our well-being through His protection, care, and provision — mirroring how a husband is called to care for his wife. It's a straightforward analogy. In a scenario where danger presents itself, the husband doesn't hesitate to confront the danger himself, prioritizing her safety above all else.

For instance, if there's a sudden noise at night, the husband doesn't nudge the wife to wake up and suggest that she confront the unknown threat. The husband's innate instinct is to shield and protect her, so he steps forward first to ensure her safety. Likewise, Christ positions Himself as our foremost protector. He acts as our shield, ensuring that nothing can reach us without first going through Him.

Verse 28: "So husbands ought to love their own wives as their own bodies; he who loves his wife loves himself."

At the heart of Paul's message is the absolute certainty that Christ's love for us is unconditional and all-encompassing. This love comes with no strings attached, no expectations of reciprocity. Paul illustrates this through the analogy of a man loving his own body, suggesting that as naturally as one cares for oneself, so should a husband love his wife.

Paul isn't encouraging a marital competition of duties or virtues between spouses. Over my fifty years in pastoral care, I've witnessed countless couples in distress, often citing this very passage from Ephesians as a weapon in their marital disputes. One spouse may accuse the other of failing to submit properly, while the other may counter with an accusation of not receiving Christ-like love. Yet, such interpretations miss the crux of Paul's teaching, reducing it to a mere exchange of accusations rather than understanding its core.

This scripture is not a battleground for pointing out flaws but a reflection on the deep, intimate union between Christ and the Church, using marriage as a metaphor. Paul, perhaps, exaggerates this analogy to convey the astounding generosity and unselfishness of Christ's love and the selfless giving expected of us, not just in marriage but in our collective identity as the Church, Christ's bride.

I hope this is resonating with you. If you've used Ephesians 5 to assert authority over your spouse, demanding submission, or if you've responded with accusations of not receiving Christ-like love, it's worth taking a step back to reconsider. You may have missed the essence of Paul's message in this chapter. The reality is that embracing the teachings outlined in Ephesians, Chapters 1-3 leads us into the kind of relationship Christ shares with the Church — one marked by total and mutual self-giving rather than a transactional exchange.

I've yet to encounter a couple practicing this full, 100% - 100 % exchange. It's often a tally of who's done what, highlighting faults and assigning blame. But when both partners give their all, that's the epitome of living out this message. This isn't about keeping score; it's about mutual love and submission, reflecting the depth and breadth of Christ's love for us and our collective response as His Bride.

In verse 33, Paul offers a concise directive that encapsulates the essence of his teachings: "Nevertheless let each one of you in particular so love his own wife as himself, and let the wife see that she respects her husband." This verse serves as practical guidance for both spouses, distilling the earlier discussions into actionable advice.

For husbands, Paul's directive implies a wholehearted commitment to serving their wives with a love that transcends limitations. This love is characterized by selflessness and mutual respect, forming the foundation of a harmonious Christian marriage. For wives, it involves honoring and respecting their husbands, giving them a place of prominence and esteem above all others. This principle seems both logical and fair.

So, if there's any doubt about regarding Paul's message through the entire chapter, he brings it back to the core: Christ loves the Church. He loves His bride. He knows no end in serving us! His love is selfless and limitless. In the same breath, he parallels this with how we, representing the Church, should prioritize Christ above everything else in our lives. Giving Him first place.

UNVEILING THE MYSTERY: CHRIST WITHIN US

Placing Christ above all else can't be achieved through our own efforts alone; it requires the empowering work of the Holy Spirit within us.

Let's bring this into our daily lives. It's one thing to understand and wrap your head around grace — the finished work of the cross, unconditional love, and everlasting mercy — but it's entirely different to actively live out these truths in the face of life's constant challenges and demands. This practical application can seem daunting, which is why I stress the importance of the foundational teachings in the first 3 chapters of Ephesians. Attempting to live out the instructions in Chapters 4-6 without being anchored in the foundational truths of our identity can lead us into a cycle of legalism and a sense of inadequacy.

> Remember, the journey through Ephesians is not about adhering to a set of rules but about experiencing transformation through Christ's love, grace, and the empowerment of the Spirit.

Galatians 1:15-16 reveals what turned Paul's life upside down and inspired much of his writing: "But when God, who set me apart from my mother's womb and called me by his grace, was pleased to reveal his Son in me so that I might preach him among the Gentiles" (NIV). This revelation — that Christ had always been in him, not merely revealed *to* him but unveiled within — became his foundation. It's this understanding that Christ resides within each believer, providing life and empowerment from within, that Paul insists should be our foundational truth.

Paul reveals the mystery: "to them God willed to make known what are the riches of the glory of this mystery among the Gentiles, which is Christ in you, the hope of glory." This revelation extends far beyond the early believers, the saints, or any select group — it reaches out to the Gentiles, those who were seen as outsiders or unbelievers, those who might not have had the "eyes of their understanding enlightened."

Paul is eager to spread the groundbreaking message that Christ resides within the Gentiles too. This perspective shifts the narrative from seeking Christ as an external entity to recognizing His presence within each individual.

Imagine the impact over centuries if this was our message to everyone we came in contact with — the quest isn't about seeking a distant Jesus or Christ to enter your heart from the outside; it's about revealing the Christ who has always resided within you. This is the good news! This is the Gospel that turns the world upside down. It isn't just an uplifting message. It's revolutionary, promising hope and glory from 'within' instead of 'without'.

This became Paul's foundation from which he built upon. Paul didn't build off his works or his efforts, although he certainly did do a lot. He understood that grace leads to action not as a means to earn or deserve but as a natural outpouring from a deeper Source. The eternal Christ within us is the wellspring, empowering us to live this life of grace.

So, as you live out from Christ, the Christ that is within you, it changes your heart, it changes your actions, it changes your motivation, it changes everything about you. And all of a sudden, His priorities and His values and His mission become your priorities and your values and your mission because you recognize that the two of you are now one.

It was from this understanding, this foundation, that Paul wrote Galatians 2:20. "It's no longer I who live, it's Christ who lives in me. I've been crucified with Christ. We're in union. He went to the cross, I went with Him. And it's no longer I who live, it's the Christ who lives in me, and the life that I now live, I

live by the power of the God, of the Christ that lives in me."
(DON KEATHLEY PARAPHRASE)

Paul further illuminates this concept in 2 Corinthians Chapter 4, verse 7, saying, "We have this treasure in earthen vessels, that the excellence of the power may be of God and not of us."

Here, Paul uses the metaphor of us being mere clay pots — fragile, ordinary, and *seemingly* insignificant — to underscore a deep truth. Our true value and strength don't stem from our capabilities or attributes but from the divine treasure housed within us. This 'treasure' — the presence and power of God in us — transforms our lives. It's not about the vessel itself but about the incomparable power it contains, ensuring that our actions, our lives, and the power we exhibit in our daily walk are reflections of God's greatness, not our own.

In verses 8-11, he continues, "We are hard pressed on every side, but not crushed; perplexed, but not in despair; persecuted, but not abandoned; struck down, but not destroyed. We always carry around in our body the death of Jesus, so that the life of Jesus may also be revealed in our body. For we who are alive are always being given over to death for Jesus' sake, so that his life may also be revealed in our mortal body." (NIV)

> **Paul's message is unwavering:** Regardless of the challenges or obstacles we encounter, the life within us — Christ's life — will find a way to manifest through us.

He acknowledges that we will face persecution, distress, and various trials, yet these will not overcome us. The essence of Paul's assurance is that come what may, we will carry in our bodies the evidence of our life with Christ, showcasing His presence in our lives.

This resilience and manifestation of Christ's life within us are central to Paul's teachings. He doesn't sugarcoat the Christian walk, acknowledging that we will have tribulation. Yet, the ultimate purpose, as highlighted in verse 11, is to demonstrate the life of Jesus within our mortal frames, transforming our earthly experiences into a manifestation of His very presence within us.

Paul connects Christ's presence in you to your thought processes, enabling you to embody the mind of Christ. This integration ensures your decisions and actions are rooted in Christ, leading to a life that genuinely mirrors and manifests His life.

10

EMBODYING THE ARMOR

Paul calls us into a life where our actions and decisions naturally align with our innermost selves, free from the burdens of striving and self-driven efforts. Through Ephesians, we uncover deep truths, guided by the Spirit of Truth, revealing our identity in Christ.

Now, it's time to walk out what we've learned. What does 'walking it out' mean? It's simply demonstrating who you are. There is no need for facades or pretending to be perfect. Haven't we all experienced the facade of perfection? We go to church, ask each other how we're doing, and hear, "I'm blessed, everything's wonderful!" when in reality there's a mess of problems and emotions inside. But grace allows us to be authentically ourselves.

If Ephesians has taught us anything, it's that living authentically, as who we are, is not only possible but encouraged. Being transparent draws others to us and, ultimately, to Christ. Our attempts at perfection can block the flow of His grace and light through our lives.

In Ephesians Chapter 6, Paul provides us with practical guidance on how to embrace our imperfections. He shows us how to navigate life's challenges in a way that allows God's strength to shine through our weaknesses. By embracing our imperfections, we become vessels of His grace, demonstrating that His glory is not best displayed in our flawless exterior but in our genuine, imperfect existence.

With the foundation laid in Chapters 1-5 and our hearts prepared, let's now turn our attention to Chapter 6.

LIVING OUT LOVE AND GRACE

Verses 1-4: "Children, obey your parents in the Lord, for this is right. 'Honor your father and mother,' which is the first commandment with promise: 'that it may be well with you and you may live long on the earth.' And you, fathers, do not provoke your children to wrath, but bring them up in the training and the admonition of the Lord."

In the opening verses of Chapter 6, Paul brings our focus to the heart of our homes, emphasizing that walking out our identity in Christ starts with family dynamics — especially the bond between children and parents. He encourages us to see these relationships as the foundation for practicing the teachings of grace and love, which he outlines in previous chapters.

Within these intimate settings, we're given the first opportunity to truly live out this message. More than anyone, our family is positioned to witness our lives firsthand, illustrating that transformation begins at home and radiates outward.

To truly influence our culture and make a tangible difference in the world, embodying the kingdom of God as His sons and daughters, it must start from within. As we grow, this transformation naturally extends to our immediate family — parents, children, siblings, and then further out to our extended family —nephews, nieces, cousins, aunts, and uncles. From there, the impact of our transformation continues to expand, reaching wider circles of influence.

Then, in verses 5 to 9 of Ephesians Chapter 6, Paul extends it outside the family and brings it into the workplace.

Verse 5: "Bondservants, be obedient to those who are your masters according to the flesh, with fear and trembling, in sincerity of heart, as to Christ."

Paul's message here is straightforward: if you're working for someone, work as if you're working for the Lord. Approach your job with sincerity, honesty, and fairness — a good day's labor for a good day's wages. He encourages working with reverence and respect, urging us to take our roles as employees seriously.

Verses 6-8: "Not with eyeservice, as men-pleasers, but as bondservants of Christ, doing the will of God from the heart, with goodwill doing service, as to the Lord, and not to men, knowing that whatever good anyone does, he will receive the same from the Lord, whether *he is* a slave or free."

Then in verse 9, Paul addresses business owners and those in charge, "And you, masters, do the same things to them, giving up threatening, knowing that your own Master also is in heaven, and there is no partiality with Him."

Paul's message encompasses the entire spectrum: from family to the workplace, addressing both employers and employees. In verse 8, he shares a powerful principle: whatever good anyone does, whether from employee to employer or vice versa, will be rewarded by the Lord, regardless of one's status.

> " It sounds a lot like karma: Give good, get good. However, it's actually a universal law — the law or biblical principle of sowing and reaping.

When you sow goodness, fairness, and integrity, you'll harvest the same. On the other hand, if you plant seeds of anger, hostility, and judgment, you'll gather those crops. Paul illustrates that our actions and their outcomes are deeply interconnected.

THE SPIRITUAL ARMOR: EMBODYING THE STRENGTH OF THE LORD

Moving on to verses 10 to 20, we reach a section of Scripture that's very familiar to many of us. It's easy to read these verses and become extremely work-minded. I'm sure I'm not the only one who has found themselves daily putting on the whole armor of God. If there were mornings I forgot to do this as part of my routine, I felt as though I wasn't properly prepared for the day ahead.

But what is Paul really saying in these verses? As we examine these verses, we'll discover that these passages are all about the

Lord's strength and the power of His might. It's not about our actions or abilities; the armor belongs entirely to Him.

Verse 10-12: "Finally, my brethren, be strong in the Lord and in the power of His might. Put on the whole armor of God that you may be able to stand against the wiles of the devil. For we do not wrestle against flesh and blood, but against principalities, against powers, against the rulers of the darkness of this age, against spiritual hosts of wickedness in the heavenly places."

It's imperative that we understand that our struggle isn't against a physical adversary or a "devil." Instead, it is a battle against the mental challenges, religious influences, and societal pressures that seek to shape us according to their norms. Despite our culture's attempts to mold us, we must remain steadfast in our identity in Christ and resist any influence that contradicts who God says we are.

In 2 Corinthians 12:7, Paul mentions a "thorn in the flesh," which he describes as a messenger of satan sent to torment him. So, what exactly was this messenger? It was those who opposed Paul's teachings, particularly the Judaizers, who followed him, spreading false ideas among the Gentile believers. These Judaizers insisted that adherence to Jewish customs, like circumcision, was necessary for salvation. This constant opposition weighed heavily on Paul's mind and caused him considerable distress.

Despite his earnest pleas to the Lord to remove this burden, Paul received an unwavering response: 'My grace is sufficient for you, for my strength is made perfect in weakness.'

This revelation was a turning point for Paul. He realized the struggle wasn't against a physical adversary but rather against the internal battles we all contend with. It's about the adversarial thoughts and accusations that often plague our minds and shape our perceptions and actions. It was from this revelation that Paul could confidently write about the armor of God in Ephesians 6, pointing us to the realization that the Lord's strength and grace are sufficient in our lives.

Let's continue in Ephesians 6...

Verse 13: "Therefore take up the whole armor of God, that you may be able to withstand in the evil day."

What's meant by the "evil day"? It refers to those times when you're confronted with something overwhelming and when doubts and fears cloud your thoughts. But here's the good news: we neutralize that with the whole armor of God.

In verses 14 and onwards, Paul outlines the armor of God: the belt of truth, the breastplate of righteousness, shoes of the gospel of peace, the shield of faith, the helmet of salvation, and the sword of the Spirit, which is the word of God. This armor isn't for physical combat; it's for standing firm in the spiritual truths and revelations we've received. It's about relying on His strength, not our own. This armor empowers us to stand not in our own perseverance but in His mighty power.

Verse 14: "Stand therefore, having girded your waist with truth, having put on the breastplate of righteousness."

Who is truth? Jesus said He is the way, the truth, and the life. Hence, we are actually girding ourselves and protecting our insides with truth. Truth covers us. And then you put on the breastplate of righteousness. Who is your righteousness? Are you your righteousness? Do you create your righteousness yourself. No, He's your righteousness. He made Him to be sin for us, who knew no sin, that we might be made the righteousness of Him, righteousness of Christ, in Him, right? It was the great exchange. We gave Him our sin, and He gave us His righteousness. So, what's covering our chest is this breastplate of righteousness.

Verse 15: "And having shod your feet with the preparation of the gospel of peace."

> The Gospel of peace: He is our peace. The helmet of salvation: He is your salvation. The belt of truth: He is Truth. The breastplate of righteousness: He is your righteousness.
>
> Do you notice a pattern here?

Verse 16: "Above all, taking the shield of faith with which you will be able to quench all the fiery darts of the wicked one."

Let's explore whose faith we're talking about here. If you refer to Galatians chapter 2 and verse 16, you'll discover that we stand in the faith of Christ, not merely faith in Christ. The King James Version articulates it best, and really captures what Paul was saying — the faith "*of* Christ." Meanwhile, the New King James Version uses "*in* Christ."

There's a significant distinction between having the faith of Christ —that is, **His** faith — versus placing our faith in Him. Personally, I'll choose His faith any day. What about you?

So, let's break it down.

- We're girded around the waist with truth — He is Truth.
- We're protected by the breastplate of righteousness — He is Righteousness.
- Our feet are anchored in peace. — He is Peace.
- And above all, we take up the shield of faith — His faith — through which we quench all the fiery darts of the wicked one.
- We secure the helmet of salvation — He is Salvation.
- And wield the sword of the Spirit, which is the Word of God — He is the Word of God.

The armor of God is all about Jesus. It's not about something we have to *put on* daily. He is the embodiment of the armor and lives in us.

Verse 18 tells us to "pray always with all prayer and supplication in the Spirit," for it is through praying in the Spirit that we align ourselves with the perfect will of God. As we continue, verses 19 to 24 mark the conclusion of this chapter. Paul closes with his signature farewell, "Grace be with you," followed by the resounding "Amen."

WE ARE COMPLETE IN HIM

In these six chapters of Ephesians, Paul's intention was to instill in the Gentile believers, who lacked a religious or spiritual foundation, an understanding of their true identity. Through his teachings, particularly in the first 3 chapters, he enlightens them about their true identity and rightful position, assuring them that they had always been in Christ, even before the foundation of the world.

Over in Colossians chapter 2, verse 8, Paul warns against adopting a false identity, cautioning the believers against being deceived by empty philosophies and traditions of men. This is precisely what the Judaizers brought with them — man-made traditions and philosophies that deviated from the truth of Christ. Paul emphasizes the danger of allowing these belief systems, theological perspectives, and religious traditions to cheat them out of the truths he had taught them. He warns against being swayed by the basic principles of the world, which often lead to a distorted perception and mindset. Instead, he encourages them to remain rooted in Christ, for true identity is found in Him alone.

So, the wrong identity stems from traditions, faulty theologies, and belief systems that mirror the ways of the world. Hence, Paul redirects their focus to the right identity — Jesus Christ. In verse 9, he declares that in Jesus dwells all the fullness of the

Godhead bodily. Then, in verse 10, he says: "And you are complete in Him, who is the head of all principality and power." Paul emphasizes that true identity is found in Jesus Christ alone. In Him, the entirety of the Godhead is fully expressed. He is both fully God and fully human, and you who are 100% human are now made 100% deity because you are complete in Him, in whom the fullness of the Godhead dwells.

If you ever question your identity, Paul simplifies it in one verse. The Christ within you reveals Himself to you as you are. It's important to clarify some misconceptions: while Christ immerses you in Himself, you still maintain your individuality. We share the same Spirit as sons and daughters of God, yet retain our uniqueness. We'Re united with Christ, one with Him, yet distinct individuals.

HIS GLORY IS OUR GLORY

Likewise, you are one with me, and I am one with you, yet we still retain our distinctiveness. Jesus said in John 17:21-23, "That they all may be one, as You, Father, *are* in Me, and I in You; that they also may be one in Us, that the world may believe that You sent Me. And the glory which You gave Me I have given them, that they may be one just as We are one: I in them, and You in Me; that they may be made perfect in one, and that the world may know that You have sent Me, and have loved them as You have loved Me."

Everything in chapters 4, 5, and 6, particularly chapter 6, verses 10 to 17, is so good! How can we religiously work out what can only be lived out through the revelation of knowing the power and strength inherent in the armor — His power, His strength, not ours?

> Let me put it this way: The Father's mind is completely made up about you! Jesus perfectly embodies the Father's unwavering thoughts about you.

Everything the Father thinks about Jesus, He thinks about you. Jesus serves as the federal head of humanity. In Him, the entirety of humanity resides — whether one acknowledges it or not, this truth remains unchanged. Jesus is above all, through all, and in all. He is how the Father sees you.

However, let me clarify a misconception. The Father doesn't view us through a Jesus lens in a way that implies He can't bear to look at us without Jesus mediating for us. Instead, you stand fully on the righteousness found in Christ. You stand fully identified with Christ, with Him living in and through you. You stand fully in your sonship, wired to reflect His nature in this world.

As Paul beautifully articulates in Colossians 3:3, "For you died, and your life is hidden with Christ in God." Verse 4 further expounds: "When Christ *who is* our life appears, then you also will appear with Him in glory."

This isn't referring to His second coming. Paul is saying that as you see Christ more clearly, you begin to understand yourself more accurately. Eventually, your self-perception will align with how He sees you — this is the ultimate goal. When Christ, who is your life, is fully revealed, we appear with Him in the same glory. His life is manifested in ours.

THE HEART'S INFLUENCE ON THE MIND

So, Paul writes to instigate a change of mind in the Ephesians, which we often refer to as repentance. He emphasizes who they are in Christ in chapters 1, 2, and 3. Then, in chapters 4, 5, and 6, he essentially tells them that now, because they understand who they are in Christ, they can live it. They can simply be who they are.

Whether you're a Galatian, an Ephesian, or a member of a specific church denomination, whenever the Father initiates a paradigm shift in your life, He always starts with transforming your mind. This transformative process paves the way for a change in your thinking.

I used to believe that if my mind was renewed, my heart would follow suit. I thought that everything would fall into place if I could acquire the right knowledge. I had it all backward. Transformation begins in the heart, not the head. But as the Spirit of Truth began unveiling the depths of pure grace, I discovered that my thinking shifted because my heart brought convincing evidence that my mind couldn't refute.

So, my mind shifted, and as it did, it renewed itself with what my heart knew to be true. Once my mind started renewing, it synced with the mind of Christ within me, planting Christ-centered seeds into my spirit. The heart has a way of drawing the mind toward truth. When you begin with the head, it often conflicts with logic and tradition.

A heart softened by love has the power to influence the mind. When your heart melts in love, you start to realize God's goodness and all He has prepared for you. You become aware of the abundant blessings He has deposited within you, even without your conscious acknowledgment or acceptance. As a result, your mindset begins to shift.

> Our heart's perception of truth deepens as we embody truth, leading to a continual shift of our mental paradigm.

Because of the insights my heart receives, my mind is in a perpetual state of transformation. I now live by the revelations that the Spirit imparts directly to my spirit rather than what I intellectually perceive.

EMBRACING THE TRUTH WITHIN

Initially, it feels like a laborious process for the heart to influence the mind. But as I gained the mind of Christ in areas like grace, the Fatherhood of God, unconditional love, and enduring mercy, everything changed. Once I saw things through Christ's perspective, my mind followed suit, and my heart overflowed with joy. Eventually, my head began to trust my heart's insights. When I received revelation in my heart, my mind quickly agreed because my heart had a proven track record of being right. This is how it's meant to work.

In fact, Paul highlights in 1st Thessalonians chapter 5 that it's God's will for us to be *wholly* sanctified, with the spirit leading, followed by the soul (mind), and then the body.

> While our culture often prioritizes the mind, we can shift this dynamic by responding to our spirit. Over time, our head will align with our heart, even though it may initially resist. And eventually, your body will follow.

The most effective, efficient, and quickest way to shift your thinking is to embrace the truth residing in your heart and spirit and allow your spirit to influence your mind. Put your mind in neutral and let the Spirit of truth work through your spirit to persuade your mind.

Now, here's the remarkable part: Once you possess the mind of Christ in an area, it can deposit Christ-centered seeds into your spirit. Then your spirit, your inner man, begins manifesting what this Christ-centered mindset has planted.

Let me share a crucial insight from King Solomon, who was renowned for his wisdom. In Proverbs 23:7, Solomon declared, "As a man thinks in his heart, so is he." In the coming days and years, as the Spirit of God continues His transformative work in your life, this verse will begin to hold great significance for you.

> If you're dissatisfied with the direction of your life, it's time to make a change within your heart. Change your heart's thoughts, perspectives, and the seeds you're planting within it. Change what your heart imagines and envisions for your life.

Be prepared for significant shifts in your belief system —
they're inevitable. Expect your theology to evolve, your convic-
tions to transform, and your heart's perspective to continuously grow. This process will rewire your brain, leading you to
think increasingly Christ-centered.

You'll be able to recognize the ongoing transformation from
heart to mind taking place within you when your heart is able
to grab hold of truth and revelation but you struggle to articu-
late it because it hasn't yet taken root in your mind.

I went through this myself when I first encountered the
message of Grace. Though I embraced it eagerly, I couldn't
express it coherently to others. It's the difference between
slow-cooking in a crock pot versus zapping in a microwave.
While the mind wants to rush, the Spirit takes its time.

Out of the abundance of the heart, the mouth speaks. You'll
sense when your heart is reshaping your mind. Sometimes,
even though I know certain truths, I refrain from teaching them
because I haven't fully internalized them. When God's revelation truly becomes part of me, I'll naturally communicate it
more effectively.

This transformation takes time to develop in your life. But when it does, you'll stand firm in your beliefs, unshaken by doubt. The challenge is to let go of old perceptions and embrace the truth revealed by your heart and spirit. Some false perceptions won't be discernible until the Holy Spirit shines the light on them. But once revealed, you'll have those "aha" moments and be able to release them.

I hope Paul's words in Ephesians challenged you to embrace the truth of who you are in Christ, and authentically live out your identity wherever you find yourself presently. There's no need for pretense; just be genuine and let your life reflect the reality of the Christ life in you.

The shifts, renewals, and transformations Paul discussed with the Ephesians are as relevant today as they were then. As we come to the end of the book, I echo Paul's words from Ephesians 6:24: "Grace be with all those who love our Lord Jesus Christ in sincerity. Amen."

ABOUT THE AUTHOR

Don Keathley is the author of seven books and President of Don Keathley Ministries and Global Grace Seminary. He is married to his wife Linda, and they have two grown and married daughters, Janell and Shawn, and four grand-children.

Don received degrees from Olivet Nazarene University and a Ph.D. from Barnham Graduate School and Seminary. As president of Global Grace Seminary, he brings over 40 years of pastoral experience and a heart to develop leaders on the cutting edge of the message of grace and the finished work of the cross.

donkeathley.com

ALSO BY DON KEATHLEY

These titles can be found on Amazon

RELIGION BUSTERS

HELL'S ILLUSION

BARKING UP THE WRONG TREE

UNHOOK THE BOOK

GRACE ON STEROIDS

GOSPEL FREE FROM DOCTRINES

GALATIANS

To contact Don Keathley please visit donkeathley.com

Printed in Great Britain
by Amazon

45524871R00126